The
Wounded
Parent

The Wounded Parent

Hope for Discouraged Parents

Second Edition

Guy Greenfield

BAKER BOOK HOUSE
Grand Rapids, Michigan 49516

To

Carole,

who loves and understands

Second edition

Copyright 1982, 1990 by
Baker Book House Company

ISBN: 0-8010-3840-5

Second printing, November 1991

Library of Congress Cataloging-in-Publication Data

Greenfield, Guy.
    The wounded parent : hope for discouraged parents / Guy Greenfield. —
2d ed.
        p.   cm.
    ISBN 0-8010-3840-5
    1. Parenting—Psychological aspects. 2. Parenting—Religious
aspects—Christianity. 3. Conflict of generations. 4. Parent and child. I. Title.
HQ755.8.G73   1990
649'.125—dc20   90-1231
                                                                                CIP

Printed in the United States of America

Contents

Foreword

Guy Greenfield is a rock which has been pounded by some harder-than-rock realities. Any average person would have chucked it by taking one of the two reactions to stress . . . fight or flight.

Since Guy and Carole Greenfield are normal, they must have seriously considered both options, but they were intelligent enough to know that there is more to facing situations than fighting and flighting. They found a third option and it is called *make a deal!* That is what this book is all about.

The current sociological pot in which we are all mutually boiling has made this generation the era of pain. That pain is nowhere more pronounced than in the walking wounded called parents.

The big kick in the pants is that nobody has said much about the utter suffering, the feeling of being used—and abused, the knee-jerk desire to kill your own kids (oh, yes!), the guilt for even harboring the thought, the hundreds of books about what we parents did to make these people we bore to be the poor things they are. No one had written much . . . until Guy Greenfield came along.

This man is a tell-it-as-he-sees-it man. And he isn't about to give you the SOS (same old stuff).

Here is a volume that offers help—real help, constructive assistance, power to cope—for the hurting, frustrated Christian parent who happened, under God, to be chosen to sire or bear a child who later tossed Christian belief and morality out of the window and has been searching for a substitute.

There are forces working on your children that seem to be mindless grinding on the basics in which most people believe.

Dr. Greenfield has done something so spiritually, sociologically, and psychologically significant that this book must be put into a few million homes.

Don't ignore this book.

Some books should be read.

This one *must* be read.

Jess and Doris Moody
First Baptist Church
Van Nuys, California

Preface to First Edition

This book is for Christian parents who have tried to center their families in the life of the church but who have become discouraged by the attitudes, beliefs, values, and behavior of their children as they have grown into the maturity of adolescence or the early adult years. The word *wounded* describes the feelings of a parent who realizes that his or her son or daughter has rejected the family's religious and moral values and has adopted a radically different lifestyle.

The feelings of a discouraged parent are usually varied. The words *hurt, angry, frustrated, confused, rejected, offended, embarrassed, used, abused, disappointed, unappreciated,* and *resentful* describe how parents may feel when their children go astray morally and spiritually.

I have tried to speak to the problem of being a wounded parent, as I have both experienced that problem personally and counseled with numerous other wounded parents. Several illustrations, which have been taken from real situations and from a variety of communities, are used throughout the book. The names, places, and identifiable information have been changed to guarantee anonymity for those involved. You may not identify exactly with any of these family experiences except at the point of the feelings, the responses, and the hunger for some answers. If so, this book can be of help to you.

Your experiences, your personal story, and your pain are unique to you and your spouse. But wounded parents share a lot in common: we hurt, both for ourselves and for our children, and we need help. We comprise a fellowship of suffering that, at times, can be very intense. We all have made our share of mistakes and struggle with guilt and anger. But we still love our children, and we want to build a new relationship with them. For many of us the future could involve a healing ministry to other wounded parents.

Therefore, I hope this book can offer to you some meaningful understanding of what has happened to you, new hope for the future with your son or daughter, significant healing for the wounds inflicted in the past, and the possibility of becoming a wounded healer yourself. After all, there are many of us.

Parents who would like further help in childrearing techniques in general or in coping with rebellious teen-agers in particular are referred to Appendix A, "Books about Parenting Techniques."

I am a Christian father of three children. My experience as a parent covers more than twenty-four years. My wife, Carole, has faithfully walked with me through many experiences both pleasant and painful, with our own children and with children of other parents.

I am a churchman who is deeply involved in the life of the Christian community. Therefore, I write from the perspective of the Christian faith, the Christian family, and the Christian church. Regardless of your denominational identity, this book is written with the hope that you can find a new meaningful relationship with God as revealed in Jesus Christ and with your son or daughter as a result of what has happened in your family in these recent years.

I would like to acknowledge several people who have contributed, either directly or indirectly, to the writing of this book. For years, my major professor in seminary, Dr. T. B. Maston, encouraged me to write. His encouragement has helped me to continue writing. Dr. Maston is now professor emeritus of Christian ethics at Southwestern Baptist Theological Seminary in Fort Worth, Texas, where he taught for more than forty years.

My own family has contributed in so many ways. Carole taught me innumerable lessons about parenthood as the mother of our children. Her love, encouragement, and helpful evaluations kept me working to the completion of this project. Her sharing with me in support groups gave me invaluable insights into personal growth and parenting. Our children, Paige, Nelson, and Todd, have been a primary source of inspiration, since they made it possible for me to learn the lessons of parenthood. Their insights and suggestions have made this book stronger than it would have been without them. Each one encouraged me to produce this book, and for that I am grateful.

I want to offer my special thanks to the wounded parents I have counseled through the years. They and their children were the initial inspiration for this book. This is as much their book as it is mine. To the White Rock Baptist Church of Los Alamos, New Mexico, goes my deepest appreciation for giving to me the wonderful privilege of being its pastor for five exciting years, during which time this book was born in the experience of ministry in that community.

Preface to Second Edition

Ten years have passed since I first began to write *The Wounded Parent*, which was initially published in 1982. The response of readers has been overwhelming. Frankly I had no idea that there were so many wounded parents, especially in the churches. The phone calls and letters from readers have been too numerous to record. Many of the readers simply wanted to share something of their continuing struggle and pain as well as to express gratitude for helping them to see some light at the end of the tunnel. Others wanted to share significant break-throughs in communication and healing in their family situation, some of which they attributed to suggestions found in the book.

I will never forget the first phone call that came from a reader. A mother called all the way from Detroit just to tell me her story. For over two years Molly had carried on a constant battle with her teenage son, Chris, then fourteen years old. His major problem was his apparent inability to get along at school, especially with his teachers and the principal. Chris has been suspended from school several times. His grades were terrible, and he seemed unwilling to cooperate with anyone in authority.

Then one day a close friend loaned Molly her copy of *The Wounded Parent*. The title itself appealed to Molly and she read the book in one sitting. Then she began to think of ways to begin putting its principles into practice with Chris. Molly soon got her chance. About 11:00 A.M. the next day the principal at Chris's school called to say that Chris was being suspended again.

As Molly drove into the school driveway, she saw Chris standing by the curb with his hands in his pockets and his head down, staring at the sidewalk, a picture of total depression. When Chris stepped into the car, Molly struggled to overcome her usual reaction: berating, judging, threatening, with angry words spoken loudly. This day it was going to be different. She decided to try a new approach based on what she had read the night before.

Molly reached over and laid her hand gently on Chris's drooping shoulder and said, "Honey, I'm sorry you're having a bad day. If you want to talk about it, I'm here to listen." Molly said that Chris suddenly turned his head toward her and with eyes wide open responded, "Mom! For real? You mean that?" Mother and son had a good cry in each other's arms. On the drive home and later in the den, Chris poured out his heart as he had never done before. Molly said she just sat there, caring with nonjudgmental listening, and it was the beginning of the healing process that was still continuing as she talked with me several weeks later. Chris had since returned to school and his behavior and grades were rapidly improving.

Responses like this one are always gratifying to an author. The stories of growth and change have been many, and each one is unique. But they illustrate that there are workable ways to cope with parental discouragement. These ways follow biblical principles that work hand-in-hand with sound psychology as it relates to wholesome parent-child relationships.

Not all of the stories that have been relayed to me have had as quick and satisfying results as the story of Molly and Chris. Some parents have seen no change in their situation. Their children are still causing them much pain and the parents are simply learning how to cope a little better. Other parents have had to wait years to see any changes.

One of my students here at the seminary told me about his neighbors. This couple, in their middle-age years, had two young adult children that had caused their parents a lot of heartache and there had been no contact with the children for over two years. The last word they had was that their son was somewhere in Texas and the daughter was somewhere on the West Coast. The parents had decided to block Jack and Jennie out of their minds because the pain their children had caused had been too much to bear.

So Phil gave his neighbors, Bob and Sally, a copy of *The Wounded Parent* to read. Sally read it the first evening. Her response was so strong that Bob read it the next evening when he came home from work. Bob and Sally began to pray for special guidance. This in itself was a break-through, since Bob and Sally had stopped going to church and praying. Soon they decided to start looking for Jack and Jennie.

Through a variety of contacts they found Jack in a county jail awaiting sentencing on a drug charge, but part of his problem was that he had gotten hooked on drugs. Bob hired an attorney and talked with the judge about possible options for Jack. The judge agreed to release Jack if he would agree to enter a drug-rehabilitation program. Jack agreed and in two months was able to come home and look for work. Bob and Sally took Jack back into their home and helped him find a job.

It took longer to find Jennie. Eventually Bob and Sally located their daughter in California. She had been through two marriages and was now divorced, had two children, and was living on welfare. Jennie was sent airline tickets for a flight home. Sally offered to take care of the children, and Bob said he would help Jennie find a job. There is much more to the story, but this was a start at rebuilding a fragmented family, and Phil told me that God used this book to turn things around.

Many pastors and church staff members, mostly ministers of youth, have told me they consistently give copies of this book to church members and others who are experiencing parental discouragement and pain to one degree or another. I stopped counting parents who have told me their "story" which resulted from reading the book.

There is a great hunger for parenting education in the churches today. Parents are literally begging for help. The American educational system, including the churches, does not have a very good track record in guiding couples in rearing their children. In the first edition of *The Wounded Parent* I recommended that churches take the lead in teaching sound parental techniques. One suggested method was the use of small support groups. Many churches have done that, using this book for guidance and discussion (see discussion questions at the end of each chapter).

I have added a concluding chapter which presents guidelines for discovering healing for the "wounded parent" malaise, including a special section for young couples with small children on how to *prevent* becoming a wounded parent.

This revision is sent out with a prayer that God will continue to use its contents to assist wounded and discouraged parents not only to find healing for themselves but also to develop insight and strength to become wounded healers of others.

1

When Your Child Goes Astray

Parents can sometimes be incredibly ignorant about what goes on in the minds and lives of their children. There is a tendency for some parents to think that all is well, there are no problems, and the family is fine, when in reality things are not going well at all. A child can leave a family and still be at home. The break can be moral or spiritual rather than physical.

The Shock of Discovery

The Wallace family was moving from Arkansas to Colorado. The father, the Rev. Arthur Wallace, had been invited to become the pastor of a young church in a fast-growing suburban community. The Wallaces were traveling in two automobiles, hoping to arrive at their new home just before the moving van would pull into their neighborhood.

Rev. Wallace was driving the lead car, accompanied by their fifteen-year-old son Roger. Mrs. Wallace (Betsy) was driving the second car, with their eighteen-year-old daughter, Susan, a recent high-school graduate.

For several days, Betsy knew that Susan was troubled

about something. The excitement of a new home in a beautiful state and a challenging church for Dad made no difference. Susan had looked obviously depressed for several days. Moreover, she had been nauseated occasionally during the past few weeks and was not eating well. Her response to Betsy's questions was, "Oh, it's nothing." Betsy had assumed Susan's problem was that she had to leave her friends behind, especially Chuck, her boyfriend.

However, halfway between Arkansas and Colorado, Susan decided she had to tell her mother the apparent truth: she was pregnant. She knew she could not hide her problem indefinitely. Betsy and Susan were driving just outside of Oklahoma City when Susan told her story. She and Chuck had been intimately involved for at least four months. She was probably two months pregnant.

For the next several miles Betsy was frozen in the shock of a staggering discovery. Questions flooded her mind: "How can I help my daughter? Will she let me? How and when will I tell her father? What will Roger think? How will Susan's grandparents react, or should they know?" Then came a big question: "How will we face a new congregation?" Before long the emotions flooded: anger, fear, resentment, pain, compassion, self-pity, embarrassment, depression.

Such situations happen more often than we realize—even to Christian parents. The situations and problems vary with each case. In one family the situation may involve drug abuse; in another, a misdemeanor or felony theft; in another, alcohol use or abuse; in another, homosexuality or premarital sexual relations; in another, arrest, and possibly jail or prison; in another, chronic dishonesty. Or a runaway son or daughter throws the family into the crisis of not knowing for weeks or months where he or she might be. Other parents face a situation in which the son or daughter gradually stops attending church and starts associating with "the wrong crowd."

When parents discover that their child has gone morally or spiritually astray, that discovery comes as an emotional injury, an injury that is often deep and painful.

Taken by Surprise

For parents who have been loyal to what they consider to be the highest moral and religious values, the discovery that one of their children has decided to break with one or more of those family values may come as a total surprise. Susan Wallace had been extremely active in her church's youth program, Sunday school, youth choir, and training classes. She appeared to be a model pastor's daughter, giving her parents very little trouble through her teen years.

Susan was known as a fine, beautiful Christian girl. But Susan was also good at keeping secrets. She told her parents only what she wanted them to know. Her relationship with Chuck had been her first intense romance. She didn't want to lose him. But Chuck was not active in church. Consequently, her relationship with him was only casual as far as her parents knew. The Wallaces never imagined Susan would be sexually involved with this boy. There was a lot they did not know.

When the complete story came out, Arthur and Betsy were taken by surprise. They were stunned and in a state of shock for the next week. It is often the case for parents to assume naïvely that such things do not happen to Christian families.

Moral Kidnaping

The Wallaces felt that Susan had been morally kidnaped. They had not reared their daughter to behave immorally. Although sex was rarely discussed at home, the Wallaces had assumed that Susan would "know better" than to have sexual relations outside of marriage. After all, the church took this position (in some of its published literature, somewhere!), and Arthur had even alluded to Christian sexual values in some sermons. Wasn't Susan listening?

The enemy was "out there" somewhere. Immediately and directly, the enemy was Chuck. After all, wasn't he responsible for Susan's pregnancy? Other segments of "enemy territory" included the high school Susan attended, and especially her peer group. The entire youth subculture tended to be sexually permissive. "They" kidnaped Susan.

Parents may carelessly blame others outside the home or the environment when their child goes astray. It is so easy, and certainly less painful, to see the cause of the problem as an invasion from without. Nevertheless, having a child go astray creates a helpless feeling. It is like having a child kidnaped. How do you get him or her back?

Fighting for Recovery

Shortly after the Wallaces moved into their new home, a physician confirmed Susan's pregnancy. She decided immediately to have an abortion. This would solve the problem for everyone, she thought, not realizing that one moral problem is compounded by another.

By a long-distance telephone call, Chuck begged Susan not to abort the child but to come back. Then, as soon as he could "afford it," he would marry her. However, Susan desperately wanted to attend college, and a baby would be "inconvenient."

Arthur and Betsy tried to advise Susan of her options: she could bear the baby to rear herself, with or without Chuck; she could bear the baby to place for adoption; her parents could adopt the child; or she could have an abortion. Any one of these options entailed serious emotional consequences. The Wallaces left the decision to Susan.

Susan insisted on an abortion. In that case, Arthur felt she should handle the expenses from her own savings. This was one decision from which he would not bail her out. In a few days Susan entered the hospital and had the abortion.

Since Chuck kept calling and pleading with Susan to return to him, Arthur decided to find out more about this young man. An investigation revealed that Chuck was on probation for a felony theft. He had been in trouble with the police several times. Susan refused to believe that this mattered.

Also, Chuck was supposedly enrolled in a state college. His parents believed he was enrolled, and regularly sent him money which was his main support. Further investigation revealed he was not a student, but only lived near the campus.

During the weeks after the abortion, Susan and Chuck rekindled their romance with almost-daily letters and long, expensive phone calls. Arthur and Betsy spent hours trying to persuade Susan not to return to Chuck. They did not know him, and what they knew of him they did not like. He was not a Christian, and lived by anything but Christian standards. Arthur became desperate to morally recover his "kidnaped" daughter. He tried to destroy Chuck's letters before she could see them. He made every effort to stop the phone calls.

One evening Arthur took the phone away from Susan while she was talking to Chuck and verbally blasted the "no-good bum" for all he had done to Susan and the Wallace family. Susan became hysterical, threatening suicide as she ran out the front door and down the street in a driving rain. Arthur went after her and brought her home in a most depressed state of mind.

In fighting for the recovery of their daughter from "moral kidnaping," Arthur's and Betsy's tactics of desperation actually drove Susan to leave home and return to Arkansas. For the next two months Susan lived with Chuck at his apartment near the college campus. However, all did not go well with them. As soon as Chuck's money from home proved inadequate for two people, he told Susan to go back to her parents, and that as soon as he could get a job, he would call for her to rejoin him. Susan returned home in disgrace, and she never heard from Chuck again. It took Susan almost two years to get over Chuck's rejection. The scars still remain.

The Initial Cover-up

The Wallaces' first reaction to the news of Susan's pregnancy was to keep it a family secret. But this was impossible. A member of Arthur's parish was a nurse on duty in the hospital where Susan had the abortion. Another church member was a physician, in the same hospital, who saw Susan's records.

What the Wallaces didn't know at the time was that both the nurse and the physician had had similar experiences with their own children.

Cover-ups usually close the door on sympathetic understanding and emotional support in such times of distress. When it was obvious to the Wallaces that trying to keep their problems secret wouldn't really work, they chose to share their problem with a small circle of church leaders and their wives. The response was one of genuine care and support. Some of the deacons had had similar, if not worse, difficulties with their children. Sharing the pain brought healing.

Resenting the Peer Group's Victory

On reflection, the Wallaces could see that Susan had begun to drift away from the family's Christian values during high school, when she chose a peer group outside her circle of friends from church. Gradually, this group of five girls became the most influential force in her life. Susan earnestly wanted to belong to a popular group of peers. In order to be accepted by these girls, she conformed to their moral standards, which represented a thoroughly secular lifestyle. Sex, profanity, alcohol, and excitement were the four major ingredients in their lifestyle.

Looking back, the Wallaces realized that Susan's peer group had successfully converted her to its secular way of life. Susan's parents' initial reaction was to deeply resent this group. How is it possible for a small group of teen-agers to undo in a few months what parents take years to build? Where does a peer group get its power to reverse a youth's value system? For the Wallaces, Susan's peer group had become the "enemy," almost without the Wallaces knowing it at the time, and the "enemy" had won.

Baffled and Confused

When parents lose a son or daughter to a moral lifestyle that opposes their own, the initial response is usually bafflement and confusion. Arthur and Betsy kept asking each other, "How could this happen to us? What would make Susan do a thing like this? Where did we go wrong?"

Parents often feel that they are doing their best under the circumstances when they rear their children. It isn't easy being parents today. It seems that previous generations knew more about how to rear their children than this generation does. The roles were clear-cut and definite. Everyone knew what was expected of them. Today this is not so.

In recent decades parents have been offered a dozen different ways to rear children. There is general confusion as to which method is best. Most of us choose an approach that seems best for us, which is usually similar to the way we were reared. Even then we often fail, or so it seems.

Why? Were we blindly inconsistent? Did we say one thing and do another? Were we short on love, short on discipline, short on communicating our values and religious convictions? In the midst of defeat, we rarely have the insight to know. All we know is that we're confused, puzzled, and have no solid answers. Maybe there aren't any. What difference, we reason, would those answers make now?

Where Was God?

For Christian parents, some of the disturbing yet inevitable questions are, "Where was God? Why did He let this happen to us? Why did He let us down?"

Parents who have honestly tried to rear their children in a Christian home where church involvement is considered natural, where Bible reading and prayer are as much a part of family behavior as eating and sleeping, where love and discipline are fairly well balanced—such parents have a difficult time when one of the children decides in both words and actions to leave the Christian faith. These parents truly feel "betrayed" by God.

It was not easy for Arthur Wallace to preach his first sermon in his new church because it was the first time to preach after he learned about Susan's pregnancy. What message did he have from God, a God who let him down? The only comforting thought he could muster was a statement he recalled from a seminary professor's lecture many years before, a question from a father who lost a son in battle: "Where was God when my boy was killed?" A friend was quoted as responding, "He was where He was when His Son died on the cross."

It was then that Arthur hoped that something redemptive and beneficial would come out of Susan's situation. At that time, however, the possibility did not seem likely. The questions still lingered. Where was God? Isn't God supposed to save us from such experiences?

Asking for Help

When your son or daughter has gone astray, one of the worst things you can do is pull into your shell and hurt. Many of us believe that such problems are so personal that they aren't anyone else's business. We think that in time we can handle our own problems. We learn from our culture that we are supposed to be able to stand on our own two feet.

This attitude may be called the Superman or Wonder Woman complex. What is wrong with this is that such an attitude is based on an unrealistic view of oneself, and it's stupid. There are no superpeople, including Christians.

When you feel your family has been torpedoed, you need help. Asking for help, although at first a difficult step for many, can be the first movement toward recovery. The Wallaces turned to an inner circle of two deacons and their wives. These couples had had similar experiences with their children and functioned as an understanding support group.

In addition, the Wallaces turned to a fellow pastor in another state, who knew the family well. A three-day visit with him and his wife helped to put matters into proper perspective. Since Susan knew and trusted him, she was able to tell things to this friend which she could not tell her parents at the time.

To ask for help is not only to acknowledge our humanity but also to begin the desired healing process. God uses other people to assist in healing in the emotional realm, just as He does in the physical realm.

The Need for Patience

The Wallaces had a long road ahead of them in regard to their relationship to Susan. It took several months to see any significant changes take place either in Susan or in themselves. Sudden recovery, instant healing, or quick solutions are rare in the areas of value differences and relationships. Such matters take time.

A particularly serious mistake made by many parents whose children go astray is the expressed lack of patience. We so often want everything to work out right immediately, or at least by the first of the month! But the reality of most situations works against this.

Susan not only had chosen a boyfriend from a different background; she also had chosen to experiment with a different moral lifestyle from that of her parents, and had found it "fun, exciting, and pleasurable." In time came the anguish of an abortion, the pain of rejection by Chuck, and the anger of her parents. Susan failed to realize that these were the results of her new lifestyle rather than the supposed poor choice of friends and behavior. Therefore, it would take time for her to see the difference.

A great need for Arthur and Betsy, consequently, was patience. God has a way of working wonders if we will give Him the room and the time to do it His way. For most modern parents, patience comes hard. We have a low tolerance for pain. We want instant relief.

It took ten years before Arthur and Betsy saw any positive results from their patience with Susan. During these years Susan floundered morally and spiritually, bouncing in and out of colleges and from one boyfriend to another, "hitting bottom" several times, even attempting suicide on one occasion. Finally by the grace of God, Susan reversed her life direction, an answer to the many prayers of many people. She returned to finish college, got a good job, and eventually met and married a wonderful man. Today she has been happily married for over four years and serves as an office manager for a professional concern. The Lord took care of her even when she was in "the far country."

Questions for Discussion

1. What were your emotions when you first discovered one of your children going astray?
2. If Susan Wallace had been your daughter, what would you have done differently from what Betsy or Arthur did?
3. Can you talk about your family situation with a small circle of friends from your church? If not, why not?
4. Why does being a parent seem so difficult today?
5. Do you feel that God has failed you in your family situation? If so, can you describe your attitude?

2

A Parent's Shattered Dreams

Our culture teaches us to dream, to plan for our children's future. Although our dreams may be somewhat unrealistic, they are important to us and contain a degree of pleasure in the dreaming process itself. However, dreams can be shattered on the reefs of reality. Things don't always turn out as we had hoped. Yet we are seldom prepared for this.

Those Early Years

Phil and Constance Fisher were extremely pleased and proud when Jeff was born. Their dreams for him included every possible ambition. They took seriously the vows they made in church the Sunday Jeff was dedicated to the Lord on parent-and-child dedication day. Surely, they dreamed, he would grow up to become an outstanding Christian person in whatever vocation he might choose for himself. They dreamed he would one day marry a Christian woman and discover the joys of his own Christian family.

These were big dreams, covering many years. Maybe it would have been enough at first just to dream of the happy days that Jeff would experience as an infant, boy, and young man before he left home. However broad or long-range the dreams, it is normal for parents like the Fishers to aspire to noble goals for their children.

Parents always desire that their children be healthy in both body and mind and that they stay that way as they grow up. Christian parents certainly dream of the day when each child accepts Jesus Christ as his or her Savior and continues growing in the knowledge of God and the Christian way of life.

The Years of Fulfillment

In time the Fishers saw many of their dreams for Jeff come true. In his preschool years he was a pleasant child who generally responded well to Phil and Constance. He received what most parents would have considered an adequate amount of love and attention. Moreover, it seemed that he responded well to the discipline of his parents.

Jeff's grade-school years seemed fairly typical. There were a few problems at school, but nothing particularly serious or long-standing. He seemed to get along well with the other children, and his schoolwork was above average. At age ten, Jeff made a profession of faith in his church, was baptized, and continued in all the activities that the church offered for children his age. He would pray at home along with all the other members of the family. He knew what it meant to own and regularly read his Bible.

By the time Jeff reached junior high school, he was well on his way to fulfilling his parents' dreams for him. The Fishers' expectations of Jeff were being fairly well fulfilled even by the time he reached high school. There were a few disciplinary bumps along the way but nothing serious.

Early Signs of Rebellion

Years later the Fishers could look back on Jeff's development and see some early signs of rebellion. They could remember catching him lying about something, but this didn't happen very often. They could recall times when he would take something that didn't belong to him. This too was not a regular thing.

The thing that bothered the Fishers the most was Jeff's growing independence. He had a mind of his own and could think for himself. This especially worried Phil when Jeff would not do exactly what he was told to do. Phil's reaction to Jeff's "insubordination" (Phil had been in the Marines) was often harsh and extreme. Phil used his belt quite often, especially during Jeff's junior-high-school years.

It seems that the Fishers failed to understand the natural process of a child growing up and cutting the cords with his or her parents. Although the cutting should be a gradual process, it does need to take place. It usually begins in the preteen years and accelerates through adolescence.

There are two possible misdirections a child can go in this process of cutting the cords. One is for the cords to be cut too soon, either by irresponsible parents or by a stubborn, rebellious child. This process would be much like a student pilot being sent up on his first solo flight so soon that he would likely end his flying career earlier than expected.

The second possible misdirection is for parents to resist cutting the cords for as long as possible. This may produce either a rebellious child (both nature and culture tell him or her to cut the cord as soon as self-confidence allows) or an excessively dependent, anxious, and fearful child who has no self-confidence. The uncut-cord people are as much a problem to society as the rebellious ones.

The so-called early signs of rebellion may actually be expressions of the natural process of growing up: achieving independence and self-confidence. The Fishers later admitted that they failed to recognize this in Jeff and overreacted with harshness and anger. They felt they would lose control otherwise.

The Invasion by the Peer Group

The peer group usually emerges during the junior-high-school years, although it may appear earlier. This group of friends of about the same age, certainly from the same grade in school, comes into a person's life in an innocent process. It is normal for a boy or girl to want friends. During the preteen and teen years the desire to belong becomes quite strong.

The function of the peer group is to assist the youth to cut the cords of the family and achieve independence. The peer group actually becomes a temporary second family, in competition with one's family of orientation (the family into which a person is born).

The major problem with the peer group comes when it represents values and a lifestyle sharply opposed to and in conflict with those of one's family. Susan Wallace chose a peer group in high school that expressed moral values strongly in opposition to those of her family. Her peer group approved of illicit sexual relations, drinking alcoholic beverages, profanity, and a disrespectful attitude toward religion. This group's summum bonum was pleasure in the context of a thoroughly secular (nonreligious) lifestyle.

Jeff Fisher also identified with a secular, pleasure-oriented peer group during his junior-high-school years. In time this group of boys began experimenting with drugs. In order for Jeff to be accepted, he had to conform to the group's behavior. One thing led to another as the pressure to belong mounted. Before long, Jeff was smoking pot and popping pills. If "everybody [the peer group] is doing it" and you're not, then what's wrong with you? To be accepted, you have to conform. In his efforts to achieve independence, Jeff discovered that he had become the unwitting victim of a new dependence, the peer group.

Unfortunately, neither Susan's nor Jeff's churches provided vital, attractive Christian peer groups. The secular, anti-Christian peer groups of the public school system had invaded the families of the Wallaces and the Fishers and had won.

Other Counterinfluences

It would be a mistake to conclude that the peer group was the only threat to Susan's and Jeff's Christian upbringing. Other counterinfluences had been at work, slowly, subtley, yet effectively.

Television is certainly a major force in the lives of today's children and youth. It has been estimated that by the time one reaches the age of eighteen today, he or she has been exposed to more than fifteen thousand hours of television viewing since birth. This is quite a contrast to the experience of this author who, although born in 1931, did not see a television set until he was eighteen, and did not own one until he was twenty-five.

The effect of television on today's youth has without doubt been tremendous. Although television is not all bad, from a Christian perspective, it has obviously presented alternative lifestyles and values for youth to consider. Much of its secular influence has been subtle. Illicit sex, the use of alcohol, and even violence often have been presented with an attitude of approval. If parents quietly condone such presentations, youth may conclude that such practices are acceptable for them also.

Magazines, books, and movies, along with the lyrics of youth-oriented music, certainly can convey messages that counter the Christian way of life. Many youth have accepted these secular messages as their own.

Another influence that has adversely affected some youth who have regularly attended church is certain disappointments in the life of the church. During her high-school years, Susan Wallace's church had a youth director who became sexually involved with one of the church's teen-agers. The exposure of his behavior played a major role in Susan's gradual disenchantment with the church. This sort of thing happens more often than church leaders prefer to admit. Although most youth survive such shocking news, some do not. It can be the final "push out the door" toward another value system.

When the Dreams Begin to Disintegrate

When Constance Fisher was cleaning out fifteen-year-old Jeff's chest of drawers one day and found a marijuana cigarette, her early dreams for Jeff began to disintegrate. Was this just a teen-age fling on Jeff's part? Was it merely the result of natural curiosity? Or did it signal something seriously wrong?

Soon after Susan began dating Chuck, Betsy Wallace had found a container of contraceptive foam in Susan's room. In answer to her mother's questions, Susan pleaded ignorance about how the container got there. She speculated that one of her girl friends left it in the room as a joke. With Betsy, as with Constance, disturbing questions flooded her mind. Is Susan telling the truth? If not, how far has she really gone with Chuck? Or is this just the result of a high-school senior's curiosity about such things? Could it be the signal of something more than just curiosity?

There's a Lot You Don't Know

Living with growing, active, curious, intelligent, and inquisitive teen-agers often presents a major problem of trust versus distrust between parent and youth. Parents want to be able to trust their children. Distrust is a painful experience. Yet many youth know that in their experimentation with life, in their testing of the moral limits of their family's values, if they tell their mothers or fathers everything they think or do, then they will be punished or restricted in their behavior.

Rather than face such consequences, youth often choose to hide the facts and keep their secrets. Besides, parents cannot monitor all the thoughts and actions of their children. The best that parents can do is to be consistent in their own behavior, as well as to trust their children to live up to the best they were taught. Even then there's a lot you don't know about your children's behavior. Your only recourse is to place your children in God's hands—God, who loves them so much more than human parents could ever love.

The Shattering and Its Trauma

When Constance and Phil received a phone call from the police that sixteen-year-old Jeff had been arrested for possession of illegal drugs and was being detained at the police department, their dreams were thoroughly shattered. It was not the end of the world for the Fishers, but their dreams were broken on the hard rocks of reality.

When Betsy and Arthur learned of Susan's pregnancy, their dreams also were shattered. In their long-laid plans to rear a wonderful Christian girl, in their efforts to guide such plans to fulfillment, something had gone wrong. It seemed that the whole endeavor of eighteen years had failed.

The trauma experienced by the Fishers and the Wallaces cannot be described in words. Only those couples who go through this know what it's like. The best that can be said by way of description is this: it hurts, it's hard, and it's debilitating. There is no feeling quite like the feeling of parental failure.

Dare We Dream Again?

Both the Wallaces and the Fishers expected their children to grow up and be like them. Their earliest dreams were dreams patterned after their own experiences and ambitions. Their children didn't turn out that way. The dreams were broken. Therefore, they wondered, dare we dream again?

It is natural for parents to want the best for their children, but the fact remains that our children are going to turn out to be what they want to be and not what we want them to be. These may be very different goals. But children have the right to decide for themselves what they will become.

This is hard for many parents to accept. They often feel that they have the age and experience to determine the direction their children should go. Yet people like the Wallaces and Fishers are learning that their personal examples of daily living are the best they can offer their children.

If the moral values and religious beliefs of parents are in any sense superior, better, or more meaningful than those of other people, then the children will have to discover this for themselves. This may mean discovery by way of experimental comparison of alternative lifestyles, painful as that sometimes is.

Getting Worse Before Getting Better

As you read this, you may be in the midst of a traumatic experience with your own son or daughter. You want and are seeking help. I hope this book helps you. But I want to warn you now: things may get worse before they get better.

You are going to need a lot of patience. You may need to radically change your usual approaches to your child. He or she may not be through testing the new and different lifestyles. Sometimes the testing has to run its course, much like a virus.

There may be days when you feel you can take it no more: a day when your son is sentenced by a court, a day when your daughter is suspended from school in April of her senior year of high school, a day when you haven't heard from your runaway daughter in more than four months and don't know whether she is dead or alive, a day when your sixteen-year-old son is visited by your church's youth minister and your son tells the minister to "go to hell" for no apparent reason other than that he doesn't want to attend church anymore.

Yes, your situation may get worse before it gets better. But, believe me, it can get better.

Questions for Discussion

1. Can you describe the early hopes and dreams you had pertaining to your children's future?
2. What were some of the early signs of your children's rebellion?
3. Are there any uncut-cord people in your family?
4. Why is the peer group such a powerful influence? Are there any Christian peer groups in your church? If not, can they be created?
5. What would you do if you found something illegal or morally objectionable in your child's bedroom?
6. How can parents prevent lying and distrust on the part of their children?
7. Should wounded parents dare to dream again or should you be "realistic" and accept what comes?

3

The Pain of Rejection

Rejection is a type of injury, and injuries hurt. Yet there are different forms of rejection: physical (running away), emotional (refusing to accept another's expressions of love), and moral (repudiating the values of one's family). Parents who spend many years of giving to their children do not understand why those children reject them in return. Much of the pain is in not knowing the reason for rejection.

The Parent-Child Divorce

When children do not live up to their parents' expectations, the experience is similar to a divorce. This is especially true when the parents' expectations pertain to morality and religious convictions. This type of divorce is an especially painful form of rejection.

Rejection by a son or daughter is always painful for parents. Harold and Connie Morris thought that they had given their daughter Melissa everything a child needed or could ever want. This included not only the things money could buy but also affection, attention, and affirmation. Being an only child, Melissa received everything her parents had to give. There was no sibling rivalry in her case.

Therefore, when Melissa chose to run away from home the summer before her senior year in high school, the Morrises were in a state of shock. This was total rejection on Melissa's part of everything her parents had taught her, of everything her parents had given her, and of all her parents' expectations for her.

The Morrises learned that Melissa had run away with her closest girl friend and two boys the Morrises hardly knew. Two days after leaving, Melissa called from a distant city to explain that she was all right but that she wanted to "taste life on the other side of the fence." She and the other three teen-agers ended up in a commune, where they lived for the next few months.

Eventually the Morrises were able to locate Melissa and bring her back home since she was underage. But she came back unwillingly. Her attitude was hostile as she accused her parents of keeping her at home against her will. Harold and Connie had lost their daughter by her own choice, and the rejection hurt deeply.

For the next year, the Morrises feared daily that Melissa would run away again if and when the opportunity presented itself. Any feelings of closeness, trust, or respect were gone. Parents and daughter still lived under the same roof but emotionally they were divorced.

The Rejection of Your Moral Code

There are several reasons why rejection is painful to parents. First of all, a wayward child has rejected the moral code of the parents. This strikes at the very heart of their identity. Who I am is largely expressed by what I believe about right and wrong behavior. My identity is also expressed in the way I actually behave. When my children reject my moral code, I feel very keenly that they have rejected me. At least, that's the way many parents react.

Morality represents a cluster of beliefs, values, ideals, and convictions about what is important in life. The moral standards I live by reflect my personal perception of life. I see life through the lenses of certain values. Since I have tried to pass these values on to my children, what they do with my values is what they do with me. You may not agree that this is the way a parent should always feel. Certainly children have a right to be themselves, and this may mean their choosing to be different from their parents.

I am not arguing that point. I am simply explaining how it often is with parents. A rejection of the moral codes of one's parents will likely be taken personally by the parents. We parents are too wrapped up in our moral convictions to separate ourselves intellectually from those convictions and not feel the emotional pain of rejection when our children disappoint us with their behavior.

The Rejection of Your Lifestyle

Most parents work hard to provide a certain lifestyle for themselves and their children. This style of life usually includes a certain standard of living, a certain level of education, certain cultural tastes (music, literature, food, clothes, automobiles, types of entertainment, manners, habits), long-term goals of achievement, a selection of certain friends in preference to other possible friends, a choice of religion and its organized expression, as well as a choice of a moral code for behavior.

Every family is a unique composition of these characteristics. Although most so-called middle-class families will have certain similarities because of their economic position, each family has its own lifestyle. Harold and Connie Morris, for example, had worked hard to achieve an above-average income, and had bought a lovely ranch-style house in one of the "better" neighborhoods of town. Both Harold and

Connie were college graduates. They drove a Mercury, not a Ford. They enjoyed semiclassical and classical music and read books from both the fiction and the nonfiction best-seller lists. Connie was a gourmet cook, bought their clothes from the "better" clothing stores, and served the "finest" wines as they entertained their guests "royally" in their home. The Morrises were members of the Episcopalian church. Their habits and manners were "impeccable." They were "cultured" people. One of their goals was to give Melissa "the best."

When the Morrises' only daughter chose to reject all of this, that rejection was interpreted as an act of ingratitude. Melissa was supposed to appreciate her parents' lifestyle. She had grown up choosing a different (and for her parents, a lesser or less tasteful) lifestyle. Melissa didn't really care for all of the material things her parents had bought for themselves and her. School was a "drag," and she had no ambition to go to college. She enjoyed that "horrible, loud, irrational" rock music, read "cheap" magazines and novels, preferred to eat junk food, wear dirty sweatshirts and jeans (never a dress), ride in "junky" cars, drink beer, smoke pot, run around with "bummy" friends, and refused to have anything to do with church.

This behavior was more than the reflection of a generation gap. The Morrises' lifestyle lacked one thing—love. Melissa thought that her parents were more concerned about projecting a specific image and maintaining their style of living than they were about her. Harold and Connie had been short on listening, caring, feeling, and understanding—at least as far as Melissa could see. Melissa felt that a lifestyle without love wasn't worth keeping. So she looked elsewhere and chose the lifestyle of her peers at school.

The Rejection of Your Church

Church means different things to different people. There are different levels of commitment, different types of commitment, different meanings to those commitments. Involvement in church life ranges from shallow, occasional attendance to deep, personal, and faithful participation.

Church membership and involvement are usually an organized expression of one's moral code and lifestyle. For most parents, their church symbolizes the best of who they are morally, and socially, as well as religiously.

Involvement in church activities for a family entails a network of friendships and other relationships of varying intensity. If something serious happens to a family, these fellow church members will know about it in time and many will want to offer support and encouragement.

However, when a child goes astray morally, he or she will also inevitably reject the family's church and all it stands for. This will be embarrassing to many parents. It is so often taken as a sign of parental failure. What will the parents say to their friends at church (especially if the child's behavior involves the police or a pregnancy)?

J. C. and Phyllis Harper had been lifelong active members of their church. J. C. was a deacon and the Sunday-school director. Phyllis was teacher of the young married couples' class. They were close friends of the pastor and his wife. They were recognized leaders in the church.

When the Harpers' son Buffy, age sixteen, was arrested for the illegal possession and sale of drugs, they were angry, frightened, and embarrassed. They had been afraid that something might happen, since Buffy had in recent months chosen to associate with boys who had no connection with any church. The Harpers actually knew very little about Buffy's friends.

At the same time, J. C. and Phyllis began having difficulty getting Buffy to attend anything at their church. He had totally lost interest. Moreover, he had become very critical of the church, pointing out its every weakness, especially the "hypocrites" there. By the time of his arrest, Buffy had rejected everything his family's church represented.

The Rejection of God

When youth reject their parents' moral code, lifestyle, and church, the rejection of God Himself is probably inevitable, since He may well represent everything they are rebelling against. This is the result of the principle of consistency. You cannot consistently break the law and wish to retain policemen among your circle of intimates. The prodigal son may have to leave his father if the son does what he himself wants to do.

God is so identified with religious, church-going parents that when youth rebel against their parents, they will probably rebel against God also. In other words, the will of the parents is the will of God. The lifestyle of the parents is a godly lifestyle. At least, this is what the children think.

This is not a carefully reasoned-out process in a youth's mind. It is usually a subconscious process of identification. However, if there are any deep-seated feelings of anger on the part of the child toward the parents, one way to strike out in anger is to reject those values, beliefs, and practices that mean a great deal to the parents. If God means much to parents whose child is rebelling, the objects of rebellion will likely include God.

The Rejection of Your Love

Most parents would admit that their love for their children is mixed with a lot of mistakes, anger, frustration, and selfishness. However, the hardest part of the pain of rejection is the thought that a wayward child has rejected your love. Rejection of love hurts and hurts deeply. At the time, there seems to be no reasonable explanation for the rejection of sincere love. Such rejection seems to be ungrateful cruelty.

Rejection of parental love is a very personal form of rejection. For someone to reject your love is to reject *you* as a person. This is difficult for anyone to take.

Doesn't everyone want to be loved? If so, then why would a son or daughter reject parental love? A partial answer might be that the love which some parents express is actually a form of conditional love, and they don't realize it.

Conditional love is just that: I love you if. . . . I love you as long as you're good. I love you if you do what I say. I love you only if you fulfill my expectations of you. I love you if you will act, think, feel, behave, believe, and worship God just as I do. You are free to choose a way of life as long as I approve of your choice. Of course, this is not true freedom.

Conditional love is sensitively detected as such by most youth, and they usually resent it. As far as they are concerned, conditional love is not genuine love. This may be the kind of love a wayward child is rejecting. If so, that rejection is understandable. Parents need objective analysis of their love to see if it is conditional. Obviously, your closest friends aren't going to tell you whether your love is conditional. They may not really know. A professional counselor will be objective.

The only kind of love worthy of the word is unconditional love. The Bible reveals such love when it reflects on God's love for us (see John 3:16; Rom. 5:8; I John 4:10); This kind of love says, "I love you regardless. . . . I love you whether or not. . . . I love you just as you are. I love you in spite of. . . . I love you, *period*."

Sometimes a son or daughter will reject unconditional love. And that rejection truly hurts. Such pain is doubly real.

The Strain on Your Marriage

A by-product of the pain of your child's rejection may be the strain the rejection produces on your marriage. Too often wounded parents turn on one another and reject each other. For example, if one parent has been strict and the other permissive, the strict parent may feel that the problem with their child would not have happened if the other had not been so permissive. The permissive parent could counter that it was the other's strictness that caused the child to rebel.

So a blame game develops. In blame games, both teams always lose. (I will discuss this further in chapter 6.) Instead of being supportive in the mutual pain of rejection, some parents strike out at each other as wounded animals sometimes do. These may be weak marriages to begin with, so the added pressure exposes a weak relationship between mother and father.

Kay and Steve Wonder experienced this when their son Marshall got involved in the drug culture in college. They felt that they had sacrificed considerably to get their son into a first-rate school: tuition, books, and room and board were expensive. For several months, the problems the Wonders experienced with Marshall's involvement in drugs took a heavy toll on their own relationship. They felt that Marshall had really disappointed them. The emotions of frustration, anger, fear, and rejection were eventually vented on each other. Before long Kay and Steve realized that their marriage was an unstable one, and if a friend had not convinced them to go to a minister (who had clinical pastoral training) for counseling, they might not have survived the ordeal.

The Wonders learned a great deal about themselves as a result of getting help. A year later they both claimed that their marriage was stronger than ever before because of counseling. Their problems with Marshall simply exposed their need for a stronger marriage. They learned how to support and care for each other rather than to be defensive and criticize each other.

A Critical Mistake

No one likes to be rejected. A parent-child divorce is always painful. In addition to the reasons already listed, there is another reason for the pain.

Sometimes parents expect their children to make them happy in ways the parents have predetermined for their children. In a sense, such parents look on their children as the main source of happiness. This is especially true of mothers. Fathers usually look to their jobs to do this for them.

Such expectations are a form of overinvestment: If my children don't make me happy by turning out as I had hoped, then there is no way for me to be happy. This is a critical mistake. Consider two reasons why.

First of all, it is a serious mistake to expect happiness to come from outside yourself, from someone else, whether children, mate, or whomever. Happiness must come from within. If you're not happy (whatever happiness means to you) don't expect someone else to make you so. Happiness, fulfillment, or joy are your responsibility, not someone else's.

Second, if you have discovered the secret of inner happiness, you will still be disappointed if your child goes astray, but you will be in a strong position to cope with the problem and to help restore a good relationship with the child in time. Christians, of all people, should know that inner happiness comes from their relationship with God through Christ—regardless of what happens to their children.

When your child goes astray, it hurts. And it's all right to hurt if you will use the pain to discover your strengths and weaknesses and to determine to *grow* thereby (I will discuss more about growth in chapter 7).

Questions for Discussion

1. Can you describe the types of rejection you have experienced as a parent?
2. Why is it so upsetting when your children reject your moral code?
3. Why does it bother parents when their children reject their lifestyle?
4. Why were the Harpers so embarrassed and distressed about Buffy's behavior? Have you experienced similar emotions?
5. Why does the rejection of parents usually include a rejection of God also?

6. Is conditional love being expressed in your home? How can you avoid this?
7. How are you coping with marital strain due to your situation with your son or daughter?

4

Managing Your Emotions

Human beings not only have the capacity to reason and to choose, but they also have the ability to feel. Emotion is a basic part of the human response to stimuli. There are various types of emotions, and these may be experienced in varying degrees of intensity, ranging from mild to severe. Emotions can have a direct effect on one's bodily functions (for example, blood-pressure changes) as well as one's behavior. It is, therefore, important for parents to understand and manage the emotional responses they make to the behavior (stimuli) of their children, not only for their own well-being but also for that of the children.

The Reign of the Emotions

When your child goes astray, your emotions tend to take over. You may experience a variety of emotions when your child seriously disappoints you by his or her behavior: anger, disgust, sadness, fear, surprise, grief, remorse, resentment, aggressiveness, embarrassment, shame, guilt, self-pity, and hurt. Usually, several of these emotions are experienced in concert and in varying degrees of intensity.

47

One of the basic functions of the emotions is survival. Certain emotions are nature's way of equipping the human personality to cope with danger, threat, or loss. Although in one sense we choose our emotions in response to stimuli, our choices are usually learned reactions that are more subconscious than conscious.

Through the years of our growth and development, we have learned, for example, to respond with grief when we experience loss. A child who runs away is a loss. The parent responds with grief. A child who breaks the law and is arrested is a moral disappointment. The parent may respond with embarrassment in the light of exposure. The family's reputation is being threatened. We perceive others as wanting to know if we agree with our child's behavior. Our embarrassment communicates that we do not agree, and is an effort to preserve the family's reputation.

However, a major problem is what might be called the reign of the emotions. That is to say, the emotions are often so intense and so mixed that sound reasoning and clear judgment come hard. Consequently, a wayward child will not be helped by an emotionally upset and distraught parent. He or she needs understanding and rapport, patience and acceptance.

It will help if as parents you can understand these mixed and controlling feelings, learn to cope with them, and even possibly discover some new emotions that can be instrumental in building a healing relationship. Some of the emotions you may need to handle during a time of parental discouragement are discussed as follows.

Anger and Resentment: How Could You Do This to Us?

When Jeff and Marge Waldowski discovered that their sixteen-year-old daughter Sally was pregnant, their initial reactions were anger and resentment. The Waldowskis owned and operated a small grocery store where business largely depended on good and friendly relationships with customers.

News of Sally's pregnancy would likely cause some customers to avoid buying groceries from the Waldowskis. At least, the Waldowskis feared this. Talk about Sally would be inevitable for those who knew the family well, and who wanted to talk about Sally's problem in front of Jeff and Marge in the store?

Jeff and Marge were incensed. Again and again they blasted Sally with, "How could you do this to us?" Their first concern was not for Sally or the baby, but what Sally's pregnancy would do to them. They were angry, and they wanted Sally to know just how angry they were. They were suffering and so should she. They deeply resented Sally for creating a threat to their business and family reputations.

It is important for parents to understand the reasons behind their anger and to discover that they have other choices for their response to a child's misbehavior.

The subconscious reasoning behind anger is this: first, I want something; second, you won't let me have it or you prevent my having it; third, that frustrates me; fourth, people who frustrate me are bad; fifth, bad people should be punished; sixth, I will punish you with my anger.[1]

The Waldowskis wanted a good family reputation (this required a morally upright daughter) which would preserve a good income from their business. Sally's pregnancy could possibly prevent that. This threat created considerable frustration for Jeff and Marge, who in turn judged Sally to be morally bad. Since morally bad people should be punished (the usual dictate of the culture), Sally should be punished by her parents' anger.

The Waldowskis had other choices in responding to Sally's situation. They could have chosen to try to understand her behavior. Why did she get pregnant? Was she seeking attention, love, a sense of importance? Was she subconsciously trying to punish her parents for ignoring her and putting

1. Paul A. Hauck, *Overcoming Frustration and Anger* (Philadelphia: Westminster, 1974), pp. 43–54.

the family business above her welfare? Or was it something else?

In addition, Jeff and Marge could have chosen to come to Sally's aid. An unmarried, pregnant teen-age girl is in trouble. She has emotions also: fear, guilt, embarrassment, remorse. She has numerous questions about what to do. The family business may have to suffer. A daughter is more important than a family business. The business can be rebuilt (if it does decline), but the pieces of a broken daughter may not be put together again so easily.

Moreover, the unborn child needs protection, care, and a loving environment into which he or she can be born.

Consequently, Jeff and Marge could have chosen the emotions of love, acceptance, and compassion, even though there would be moments of disappointment, shame, fear, anger, and sorrow. Anger was not their only choice.

Embarrassment: What Will Others Think?

Embarrassment may be a part of the reason for anger. The Waldowskis may have been so embarrassed about Sally's situation that embarrassment played a major role in evoking their anger.

Embarrassment is a form of public shame. We in American society are so often controlled or directed by others' expectations. If we fail to meet those expectations (especially in matters of morality), we may experience shame, disgrace, or embarrassment. Failing to meet others' expectations may be seen as a type of moral failure.

Since, in American society, failure is apparently the unpardonable sin, moral failure may produce a feeling of shame or embarrassment on a deep level. The Waldowskis felt that not only was Sally a moral failure but also that they were failures as parents. Consequently, the question they kept asking themselves was, "What will others think?"

The fact of the matter is that a lot of people aren't going to think much at all. They have their own problems to worry about. Some may think the worst and withdraw whatever "friendship" they had. But some other people are going to think in compassionate, helpful, and understanding ways. Some have experienced the same problems you are now undergoing. They will be supportive if you will let them be supportive.

In the long run, it really matters little what others think. If they think the worst, then that's their problem. The most important thing is what your wayward son or daughter thinks. He or she may be thinking, "What a fool I've been," or, "Will Mom and Dad stop loving me? Where do I go from here? Does anybody really care about me? How can I ask for forgiveness?"

Embarrassment about something morally wrong that your child has done is a form of selfishness, an overconcern for yourself and an underconcern for the son or daughter. There's a message in your child's behavior. Did you understand it, or did you overlook it in your overconcern for what others think?

Self-pity: I Want to Cry

Another form of selfishness is self-pity. Karen Johnston, a divorcée, felt overwhelmed by self-pity when the school principal told her that her twelve-year-old son Robby had stolen fifteen dollars out of the petty-cash drawer in his office at school. Robby was caught in the act by the principal's secretary, who walked in unexpectedly.

Karen's husband had deserted her for another woman two years before. With no education or training, Karen had to take a low-paying job. There were two other children to care for. She already felt a lot of self-pity. Then Robby was caught stealing. This seemed to be the last straw. Karen's only response was, "I just want to cry. I don't know what else to do."

Self-pity can be an overwhelming, debilitating feeling. It can produce a deep form of depression. Feeling this way, and with no husband to support her, Karen needed to turn to some other people for understanding and advice: the principal himself, the school counselor, a pastoral counselor, a trained minister, a child-guidance-center counselor, or a family doctor.

There are no solutions in self-pity. Other people are available to help. You need not solve a problem alone. Your child's welfare is more important than your feelings of self-pity. Ask for help, not pity.

Grief: I Could Handle Death Better Than This

Grief is a response to loss. When Art and Betty Collins learned that their seventeen-year-old daughter Irene was regularly drinking a variety of alcoholic beverages it was bad enough, but during the last month of Irene's senior year in high school her parents learned that Irene was all but an alcoholic. She had been able to hide her drinking from her parents for the past two years, since they were very busy and often away from home. When Irene went to the family doctor for treatment of a viral illness, the truth came out. The doctor advised immediate action.

However, Irene's peers had the same problem as she did, and their influence was quite strong. She was not about to break off from her friends. Irene's addiction to alcohol would not be broken by her parents' condemnation. One drunken scene after another followed Irene's graduation from high school. Art and Betty tried their best to get Irene to go to meetings of Alcoholics Anonymous, but she refused.

The following months were extremely difficult for the entire family. Art and Betty felt helpless and saw the situation as futile. They had lost their daughter to the addiction of alcohol. Their prevailing emotion was grief. As Betty said, "I could handle death better than this."

Fortunately, the Collinses found a church whose clinically-trained pastor was leading grief-therapy sessions for those who had recently experienced some type of deep loss:

the death of a loved one, divorce, or an experience like the Collinses had with Irene. Art and Betty learned about the various stages of grief—shock, emotional release (crying), preoccupation with the loss, symptoms of physical distress, depression, guilt, anger, withdrawal, a realization that withdrawal is unrealistic—and how to cope with each stage. They also learned how to resolve grief—the readjustment to reality.[2] Eventually they were able to persuade Irene, who by then was desperate, to join an alcoholic-recovery group at the community mental-health center. In time her addiction was arrested.

Having learned how to handle their grief, Art and Betty were better prepared to offer supportive encouragement to Irene, which in time helped to motivate her to join the alcoholic-recovery group.

Pain: How Could You Hurt Us So Much?

Pain results from feeling rejected. Feeling rejected by a son or daughter makes a parent hurt emotionally. This is a pain that is as severe as physical pain. Most of us have experienced what is commonly called "hurt feelings."

Pain also results from feeling disappointment. High expectations for a son or daughter can be easily shattered by his or her refusal to meet those expectations and a decision to go his or her own way (especially when such behavior involves actions contrary to the parents' moral standards).

If it is true that we tend to choose our emotions,[3] then when I experience emotional pain it is because I have chosen to hurt. No one else can hurt my feelings. I choose to be hurt. When my child rejects me or my way of life (including values or beliefs), it is only natural to feel disappointment, even discouragement. But it does no good to counter with,

2. Granger E. Westberg, *Minister and Doctor Meet* (New York: Harper and Brothers, 1961), pp. 99–103.

3. Compare Albert Ellis and Robert A. Harper, *A New Guide to Rational Living* (Englewood Cliffs, NJ: Prentice-Hall, 1975), pp. 18ff.

"How could you hurt us so much?" This is only a futile effort to manipulate the son or daughter into following the parents' standards.

It's all right to hurt (to be disappointed) if you will go beyond the hurt to serious efforts to listen, to understand, to care, to support (if wanted), and to love unconditionally. More important than your hurt feelings is your son's or daughter's freedom to make his or her own decisions, even if you disagree with those decisions. If the decisions, in your estimation, are poor ones, then let the consequences be the ultimate teacher. This is not easy to do; it may be part of the pain of being a parent. But (especially for an older teenager or young adult) it may be the only way.

Guilt: This Is Somehow My Fault

A common emotion for parents to experience when their child goes astray is guilt: this is somehow my or our fault. This is the result of my or our parental failure. We were sorry parents.

As parents we all make a lot of mistakes. Our society makes no concerted effort to teach each new generation of adults how to parent. We usually parent as we were parented, or by a slight revision of such. Therefore, it may be a miracle that any of us do as well as we do in rearing children.

The temptation for some parents to play the blame game is very real. To blame oneself is rarely, if ever, a productive experience. After all, our children are responsible for their own decisions. Certainly parents have a great deal of influence on their children. But when we have tried to do what seems to be our best (although who really does his "best" in anything?), and a child chooses to go astray, then what earthly good does it do to give ourselves, as the parents of that child, a hefty guilt trip?

We can all try to learn from our mistakes and from the experience of our son or daughter rejecting our values. But a guilt trip is usually a useless form of self-punishment that often fails to teach us anything.

Fear: I'm Afraid of What Will Become of You

It is normal to be fearful of what could happen to your child, especially when he or she engages in dangerous behavior (drug abuse, alcohol abuse, criminal behavior, promiscuous sexual activity, or speeding). When your children are seventeen to twenty-five years old and behave carelessly and stupidly, there isn't much that you can do about it. Even fifteen- or sixteen-year-olds are often out of our control if they really set their minds to act foolishly.

A serious aspect of this fear is when it gets out of control, and the child knows that and uses the fear to manipulate the parents. Fear can also immobilize you, and prevent you from being the kind of supportive parent your son or daughter may need.

If a young person is really determined to harm or destroy himself, there likely isn't much you can do about it. However, you have choices other than fear. You can trust. There were times when I worried myself almost to death over our children. It was an exhausting experience. Then I learned to trust God to take care of my children. There was a day when my wife and I consciously placed our children in the hands of God. He gave these children to us in the first place. Surely He was capable of taking care of them. Besides, doesn't He love them more than their parents do? Of course. What a relief this was.

Every time fear tries to get another foothold in my life as a parent, I recommit my children into the hands of their heavenly Father. That's a safe place to be, come what may.

Choosing Your Emotions

I don't mean to sound as if managing your emotions is easy. It isn't. It is difficult. These undesirable emotions I previously discussed tend to reign, to take over our person-

alities when we're under the stress of our children's misbehavior and/or rejection of our moral values or religious
beliefs.

We choose emotions such as fear and anger because we
learned that this is the way to protect ourselves and our
families from harm. These are the ways to survive. However,
I hope at this point you are seeing that you have other
choices—productive emotions and responses to difficult parent-child situations.

Listening and understanding are better than anger and
resentment. Unselfish concern for your child's problems is
better than embarrassment. Asking for help is better than
wallowing in self-pity. Resolving grief is better than sinking
into it. Pain needs to be transcended by unconditional love
in an atmosphere of freedom. Learning from our mistakes
is better than indulging in a guilt trip. Trust in God is better
than the paralysis of fear.

The Search for New Emotions

I am inviting you as a wounded parent to search for new
emotions. There is an intellectual dimension to this search—
knowing what your options are. However, there is also an
experiential dimension. No one can do the work for you. You
have to experience these new emotions for yourself.

The new and healthy emotions I am referring to are joy,
acceptance, love, trust, compassion, optimism, anticipation,
pleasure, and triumph. I would suggest that you seriously
examine the resources of the Christian faith, especially in
the context of a vibrant Christian community of believers.
This comes only through personal involvement in a group
of caring people. Remember that trying to find these new
emotions by reading the Bible or a book about the Christian
faith is like trying to learn how to swim by reading a book
about swimming.

There is an abundance of Christian parents who have discovered that these new emotions can build or rebuild whole-

some and lasting relationships with children who have chosen to go astray. More specific steps on how to choose these healthy emotions will be suggested in chapters 7 and 8.

Questions for Discussion

1. Do you understand your emotions?
2. With which emotions discussed in this chapter do you most identify?
3. Besides anger, what were the choices the Waldowskis had in responding to Sally's situation?
4. How can parents handle embarrassment about their children's behavior?
5. Do you identify with the stages of grief the Collinses worked through? At which stage are you? How are you coping?
6. Do you agree that we tend to choose our emotions? Do you agree that we choose to be hurt?
7. How can your Christian faith help you to choose new and healthy emotions?

5

When Other People's Children Turn Out Well

Wounded parents may sometimes be overly-sensitive to what happens to other people's children, especially if those children appear successful, happy, and morally upright. Apparent "losers" are very much aware of the apparent "winners." Feelings of jealousy, even resentment, may prevail. It is so easy to get caught up in the process of comparing, and the resultant pain is never easy to handle.

The Pain of Comparing

Part of the pain of being a wounded parent is the pain of comparing your children, who have not turned out so well, with those of other families who, so it seems, turned out just as you had hoped your children would.

This is especially painful for parents who have tried to live a faithful Christian life, have been actively involved in the life of a church, and have sought to pass on to their children the values and beliefs of the Christian way.

Charles and Marilyn Martin had reared three children, two sons and a daughter. During all of their years at home these children had never given their parents an ounce of trouble. Well-adjusted, active in school and church, popular with other youth with high moral values, the Martin children were known as "some of the town's finest."

Within a span of seven years, following graduation from high school, all three of the Martin children had married and had been divorced. For Charles and Marilyn these were a most discouraging and painful seven years. They suffered through each divorce, seemingly hurting as much as did each child. The two sons had attended a small denominational college and had met their wives there. The daughter had married the son of a minister in the town where the Martins lived.

No one would ever have thought that the three Martin children would be divorced in a short time. People who rear and educate their children as Charles and Marilyn had done aren't supposed to see their children's marriages fail. That's not the way the religious culture writes the script. Nevertheless, it happened. It happens to many families these days when the divorce rate is higher than it ever has been.

One of the most painful aspects of this story is hearing Charles and Marilyn talk about the other youth who grew up alongside their three children, many from outside the church, who seemingly have had successful marriages. They want to know why their children's marriages failed while others with less or no influence from the Christian faith have had successful marriages. Again, there is no easy answer.

Each marriage is unique. There is no general explanation for why some marriages fail. Moreover, it's not fair for parents to blame themselves, or anyone else, for their children's broken marriages. The blame game is never productive.

The game of comparing is also never productive. You probably don't know the whole story in each case anyhow. Your children may have been hasty and careless in choosing a mate and did not really work hard to make the marriage succeed. Others may have succeeded simply as the result of the unmerited grace and power of God in their lives, something you may not have known about. There could be a hundred different other reasons. Still, comparing your children's situation with that of others is fruitless and painful. Don't do it. You don't have enough information to do a good job of it. Your energies need to be spent elsewhere.

Feelings of Jealousy

Probably the strongest emotion the Martins had to deal with was jealousy. They thought that they had done everything possible to produce three healthy, well-adjusted children whose marriages would be happy and fulfilling. But it didn't work out that way.

Charles and Marilyn often wondered why a certain neighbor, who was the same age as their older son, had married and seemingly was happy. Yet this man's parents had divorced some years ago, his mother had remarried a man few people liked, and no one in the family had anything to do with the church. This neighbor married a woman from even less fortunate circumstances than his own. Why were these people able to make a success of marriage, while the Martin children weren't? Charles and Marilyn became jealous, even resentful. Their resentment was probably aimed more toward God than toward anyone else. Why would He bless a non-Christian family and not theirs, they reasoned? After all, hadn't they done everything that the church taught would produce well-adjusted, happily-married children? For them, they felt, it didn't work. God didn't pay off as the church promised. A lot of people reason this way.

Why Can't You Be Like Them?

A deadly trap for wounded parents to fall into is to use the example of other people's "good kids" against their own children: "Why can't you be like them? Why do you have to disappoint us so much? Other people's children don't act the way you do!"

Robin and Jack Stevens's seventeen-year-old son Richard

had had a series of confrontations, mostly involving traffic violations, with the local police. The Stevens's next-door neighbors had twin sons, Ronald and Roger Marks, who were Richard's age and who were as fine a set of boys as anyone could want. They were never into trouble at school or with the police. Both were, you guessed it, Eagle Scouts.

But the Stevenses were constantly using the Marks boys as examples of how Richard should behave. What Robin and Jack failed to realize was that each time they did this ("why can't you be like them?") Richard deeply resented it. He wasn't Ronald or Roger. He wanted to be his own self. The comparison actually served to drive Richard further into rebellious and illegal behavior.

You can't make your children into someone else's image. You have to give them the freedom to be themselves. When they do engage in foolish behavior, as Richard did, you as parents can, first of all, try to understand the cause of the behavior (attention-seeking, for example); second, let them experience the consequences of their behavior (traffic violations result in fines or loss of driver's license); third, establish a mutually-agreed-on and fair set of rules by which you live (abuse of car privileges means loss of the keys this week or this month); fourth, try to talk about the cause of the problem and possibilities for solutions in calm, rational language; and fifth, make sure you are living by your own rules.

But throwing the "good" example of other children up to your own "bad" children is like a husband trying to tell his bride what a great cook his mother is. It just won't work. It creates resentment.

Rejoice with Those Who Rejoice

When your children have disappointed you, and they have broken traces and rejected your moral values and religious beliefs, you can easily look around and find several examples of children who didn't do that. They turned out as you wished your children had. It will be a serious mistake for you to sink into jealousy and resentment. You will only hurt yourself more and possibly create a barrier to ever rebuilding a healthy relationship with your own children.

You will do much better to rejoice with those who rejoice. Be grateful that in these days of shifting values, a time of great difficulty in rearing children (was it ever easy?), there are some parents who feel doubly fortunate that their children turned out as well as they did. You just might be able to learn something from them.

If these parents have good communication with their children, get to know them well enough to find out their secret. You may not be able to detect any difference, but if you do, that information will be worth knowing. You may learn something about yourself (for example, that you are overly-critical, a negative thinker, pessimistic, or have shallow religious faith or superficial values) that you can now see prevents good communication with your children.

But you can't learn these things if you retreat into jealousy and resentment. Rejoice with those who rejoice over their children and they will come to your aid and possibly become a supportive influence in your life.

Weep with Those Who Weep—You're Qualified

Look around you. As a wounded parent, you are not alone. There are lots of us, in and out of church. Many are the stories that could break the heart of any sympathetic listener. Some suicides of those over age forty are the result of being a wounded parent. These are people who can no longer bear the pain. Some divorces of people over forty are the result of being a wounded parent. These are people whose experiences with their children caused them to turn against each other, and the strain on the marriage was too much. They blamed each other for what their children did and in time destroyed what love they had for each other.

Wounded parents need each other. The temptation to engage in self-pity as we look at other people's children who turned out well must be resisted. There is healing for both yourself and others when you choose to weep with those who weep. After all, as a wounded parent, you are qualified. You, of all people, can understand those who are going through similar ordeals with their children. Specific suggestions about how this can be done in healthy and constructive ways will be mentioned in chapter 10.

Questions for Discussion

1. Are you caught up in the pain of comparing?
2. How would you have counseled the Martins if they had sought your advice?
3. How can parents cope with feelings of jealousy?
4. Can you honestly rejoice with those parents who are rejoicing?
5. Do you know of other wounded parents who need you? How can you make yourself available to them?

6

Looking Back—
What Went Wrong?
And What If . . . ?

Many parents want to learn from their mistakes. It is natural for us to look back and wonder, "What went wrong? What were our mistakes?" However, if we are not careful, we will ask, "Who is to blame for what went wrong? What if you had done your part in assuming parental responsibility? What if you had stayed home more? What if you had not nagged so much? What if . . . ?" We can either point a finger or do something about ourselves in the present.

Playing the Blame Game

I have already mentioned the dangers of playing the blame game. Because this is such a prevalent practice among wounded parents, I think it needs further attention. On discovering Susan's pregnancy, Arthur and Betsy Wallace soon found themselves embroiled in the game of each blaming the other for Susan's behavior. Arthur was especially prone to blame someone or something whenever an unfortunate situation developed. As a minister, he could not admit that he himself could have made any mistakes with his daughter.

"Ministers are supposed to be perfect," so dictated his culture, and Arthur felt he had to live up to that standard.

For several years, Betsy and Susan had had what seemed to have been more than their share of mother-daughter spats. Both were headstrong females who could easily become locked into a power struggle. Arthur was quick to point out to Betsy that someday Susan would go beyond mere verbal combat and do something foolish "just to get even." Arthur could now say, "I told you so." And he did.

Betsy countered in self-defense: "If only you had spent more time with us at home instead of always being at the church or out of town on speaking engagements or conferences, this would never have happened." One accusation was countered by another. Neither appeared willing to assume any responsibility for what happened. Neither considered the possibility of the cause or causes lying somewhere else, such as in Susan's own choices of friends, lifestyle, and behavior, which had little or nothing to do with what her father and mother did or did not do.

Phil and Constance Fisher also allowed themselves to become trapped in blaming each other for Jeff's involvement with drugs. Constance immediately laid the blame for Jeff's problem on Phil's ambition to move up in the company's ranks. If Phil had not taken this new position and moved the family to this particular city, then Jeff would not have been in this high school where he met this particular group of friends. If only we had stayed where we were and had not moved here, none of this would have happened, argued Constance.

In response, Phil accused Constance of becoming overinvolved in social clubs, community activities, and church, to the point that she had neglected her duties as Jeff's mother. If she had stayed home more and had been a better mother to Jeff, he would never have felt a need to experiment with drugs, reasoned Phil.

Both the Wallaces and the Fishers soon discovered that

playing the blame game is a losing situation for everyone involved. No one wins. Such a game is extremely counterproductive.

Staying Out of the Blame Game

When your son or daughter has rebelled against your Christian beliefs and values, it is normal to look back over the years and ask yourself, "What went wrong?" But instead of asking, "Who's to blame?" or "Whose fault was it?" it is so much more productive to ask, "What can I learn from this? How can I best relate to my child now that all of this has happened? How can my husband or wife and I work together in building a new relationship with our child?" In other words, stay out of the blame game at all costs.

Staying out of the blame game is not easy. We are so often prone to defend, protect, or cover up our wounded egos. For many of us, it is painful to admit that we made some mistakes in rearing our children. This is especially true of women. One of the most difficult thoughts for an American woman to entertain is, "I was not a good mother." She will do everything possible to avoid facing that reality. However, the truth of the matter may well be that the child's behavior may not be the result of bad parenting at all.

And yet what is wrong with a wounded parent admitting that he or she is not perfect and that several mistakes were made in the rearing of one's children? Who said we had to be superparents? I personally found it to be a great relief the day I discovered that my undershirt does not have a large monogrammed *S* on the front of it. Likewise, there is no large *W* on my wife's clothing. I am not Superman and she is not Wonder Woman when it comes to parenting. The day we both accepted that fact was a day a heavy burden was lifted.

There are no perfect parents. It is best to be honest. My wife and I made some mistakes in bringing up our children, and some of those mistakes possibly contributed to some of our children's bad choices along the way. What amazes me is that, when I inventory all the mistakes I believe I made as a father, my children made many good choices in spite of my mistakes with them and fewer-than-expected bad choices because of my mistakes. They survived me better than I deserved.

On the other hand, not all of the decisions my children made were due to my parenting or that of their mother. Actually, my wife and I are not responsible for what our children make of themselves. They are responsible for their own decisions. This applies to every family. In the stories mentioned previously, Susan, Jeff, Melissa, Buffy, Marshall, Sally, Robby, Irene, and the Martin children must all bear the responsibility for their choices that resulted in their respective experiences. They cannot blame their parents for what they chose to do with themselves. The blame game does not work for children any more than it does for parents.

Avoiding the "What if . . ." Guilt Trip

In addition to staying out of the blame game, wounded parents need to avoid the "What if . . ." guilt trip. When your child goes astray, there will be a strong temptation to survey the past years and punish yourself with such thoughts as, "What if I had been a better mother or father? What if we had not moved into this particular neighborhood or put him or her in that particular school? What if I, as a mother, had not gone to work but had stayed home? What if we had been more strict? What if we had been more lenient?" The "what ifs" can be endless.

Such questions are not only a form of self-flagellation but also are nonproductive and a waste of mental and emotional energy. Such mental searching goes nowhere. It is a guilt trip. You are assuming full responsibility for what your son or daughter has done or become. You may be partially responsible in some ways. To the degree that you can recognize those mistakes, confess them to God, to your child, and to your spouse. Then accept their forgiveness and be done with it.

How do you confess your perceived mistakes? The Bible has much to say about confession, pertaining both to confession to God and to others. See Psalm 32; Proverbs 23:13; Matthew 5:23–24; James 5:16; and I John 1:9.

God's forgiveness is clearly promised and eagerly offered. Confessing your perceived mistakes to your son or daughter is not so easy. Timing and place will be important. Only God, working through your good common sense, can impress you to know when and where that will be. But do confess your mistakes to your child. However, do not expect your child to readily respond in kindness and forgiveness. He or she will need time and some maturity to know how to respond. Someone has to take the first step in reconciliation. When you do your part, leave the response in the hands of God and in the will of your child. Be patient.

Learning from the Past

Instead of engaging in the fruitless search for who is to blame for what went wrong, why not try to learn from the past? Arthur and Betsy Wallace decided that the present and future were more important than the past. They realized that if they were going to have a meaningful relationship with Susan in the years ahead they would have to avoid expressing a judgmental attitude toward both one another and Susan. More importantly, they believed that somehow they could learn a great deal about themselves by carefully analyzing and patiently discussing with each other their relationship with Susan over the past few years. From this understanding, they felt that they could better relate to their daughter, perhaps building a new and stronger relationship with her.

Through working with a competent pastor friend (one trained in clinical pastoral education), the Wallaces gradually recognized several helpful, although sometimes painful, truths about themselves, about Susan, and about parent-child relationships in their family. In their case, it helped for Susan to participate in the counseling, although she met with the counselor privately most of the time.

First of all, the Wallaces learned that Susan had developed a poor self-image. Some of this was due to her physical size. She was always much smaller than her peers, and often was mistaken for being three to five years younger than her actual age. Instead of viewing herself as petite, she chose to perceive herself as the runt of the family. Consequently, Susan believed herself to be ugly, unlovable, even rejectable. Actually, most people considered her beautiful. But it is self-perception that really matters.

Second, Susan (and her parents) discovered that subconsciously she had for some years been blaming God for making her so small. If God made her so small that she was rarely asked for a date, so immature-looking that most people saw and treated her as a child rather than as a young woman, so "ugly" that no one would love or accept her, then He must not be a loving God who had her best interests at heart. Therefore, she chose to reject such a God and the standards of morality identified with Him. Susan's behavior reflected the anger she felt for what God had done to her physically.

The Wallaces also learned much about themselves: that the regular arguments, disagreements, and generally unhappy atmosphere reflected in their marriage contributed to Susan's desire to look for happiness in alternative life-styles outside the value system of her own home; that they had been more judgmental than nurturing toward Susan; that they had favored her brother Roger most of the time, causing underlying resentment in Susan; that they were often so busy at the church that Susan felt neglected at certain crucial moments in her teen years. When she wanted to share joys or sorrows, no one at home seemed to have time for her.

Arthur, in particular, discovered that his own occasional sense of vocational frustration (and what minister has not felt such?) had unwittingly been projected onto Susan for no special reason. In other words, he sometimes took his own frustrations out on Susan by harsh and overbearing restrictions. This was later reversed when Susan became a high-school senior because Arthur, in seeking to regain her love, allowed her to do whatever she pleased. Such fathering produced moral confusion for a developing young woman. Susan interpreted this to mean that the standards at home really did not matter.

Betsy learned that she, too, had allowed her personal frustrations to contaminate her relationship with Susan. Both Betsy and Susan were the older children in their respective families of orientation and therefore tended to get into power struggles. Each felt the need to prove, "I'm in charge; after all, I'm older; I'm expected to be the boss." In addition, Betsy felt that Susan had to be a "perfect" child or else Betsy would not be a good mother. Consequently, Betsy tended to be overbearing, demanding, and perfectionistic in her relationship with Susan. In rejecting her mother's control, Susan rejected her mother's faith and moral values as well.

There were other aspects involved in Susan's pregnancy and rejection of Christianity. But the Wallaces felt that in rebuilding their relationship with Susan, they had to face up to and learn from the way they had related to her in the past. They discovered many changes that needed to be made in their own lives before they could expect any changes in Susan's behavior and attitudes. Someone has to take the first step in changing relationships. The parents are the logical ones to do this.

The Unblessed Child

You have probably recognized that Susan Wallace was what might be called an unblessed child. Her parents were shocked to discover through the counseling sessions that she had grown up feeling unloved, unwanted, and unblessed. Arthur and Betsy sincerely believed that they had adequately loved their daughter through her developing years to the present. And they probably did, in the only way they knew how. But what mattered most was Susan's perception of her parents' attitudes and behavior toward her. As far as she was concerned, she was an unblessed child.

The Bible speaks of parents blessing their children. It also reflects the custom of prominent figures, such as rabbis, blessing children. The story about Isaac and his sons, Esau and Jacob, has this practice as its backdrop in Genesis 27–28. (See also Gen. 48:15–49; Deut. 33:1; Mark 10:13–16; Luke 18:15–17, where Jesus blessed the children brought to Him; Eph. 1:3, which notes that God blesses His children; Heb. 11:20–21.) This practice in Bible times involved specific purposes related to the passing on of leadership and property, as well as a sort of prophetic expectation pertaining to the child's future. It also implied important psychological influences on the child: acceptance, trust, and encouragement. A child who is not blessed with these endowments will have difficulty developing a strong and positive self-image.

It has been my observation that children who grow up in Christian homes and eventually go astray tend to see themselves as unblessed children. Their rebellious and wayward behavior may be a form of subconscious communication. The message is, "Since you [the parents] did not bless me, then I will curse you by my actions." That is one possible explanation.

Another explanation is that the wayward child seeks to be blessed (accepted, trusted, loved, encouraged) outside the family, perhaps in a peer group. In so many instances the peer group reflects a value system and lifestyle contrary to that of the Christian home of the seeking youth. In order to be accepted by the peer group, he or she must conform to the values and beliefs of the group. Unblessed children will often pay the price of violating their Christian values if they believe they will receive love and acceptance in return. People who feel unloved will often pay any price in order to feel loved.

Parents of an unblessed wayward child need somehow to make up for lost time and bless that son or daughter. This will not be easy. Your first efforts may be met by rejection or cynical resentment ("It's a little late, don't you think?"). Actually, there is no way to make up for the past. You can only attempt to redeem the present. But it's worth the try.

Acceptance, especially at a late date, must be unconditional. You don't have to compromise your own moral convictions, however, to do this. You can accept a son who is taking drugs without allowing him to bring them into your house. You can welcome your son and his girl friend (who lives with him) into your home and still arrange for them to sleep in separate bedrooms during their visit. It is *your* house. You can enforce the rules of the house and still accept your child. Acceptance is more attitudinal and behavioral than it is verbal. Acceptance avoids judgmental condemnation. Acceptance communicates the fact that you value him or her as a person of infinite worth, regardless of his or her behavior. It is seldom too late for such a blessing.

Looking Ahead

Don't dwell on the past. What has happened has happened. Laying the blame on another is neither your business (you are not omniscient) nor a productive procedure. Avoid berating yourself for your "parental failure." Jesus died for our sins. We need not nor cannot atone for them. Learn from the past as best you can (although our memories and perceptions are often poor). Reach out to bless your child as best you can at this late date with love, acceptance, trust, and encouragement.

However, your primary orientation should be toward the future. Look ahead toward developing a meaningful relationship with your child, whether he or she is sixteen, twenty-six, or forty-six. The God revealed in Jesus Christ is a God of reconciliation. He knows a great deal about how this can be done. His reconciling resources are unlimited. The remaining chapters in this book will explain these possibilities.

Questions for Discussion

1. Why are some parents prone to play the blame game?
2. Can you recall recent examples of your blaming some-one else for what happened in your family?
3. Do you feel an inclination to put up a pretense of per-fection? Why?
4. Do you take the "What if . . ." guilt trip? Why?
5. What constructive lessons can you derive from the past in regard to your children?
6. Is there an unblessed child in your family? What can you do about this?

7

Overcoming Discouragement

In time, a wounded parent becomes a discouraged parent: one "deprived of confidence, hope, or spirit," as the dictionary says. The word *discouragement* literally means "the state of having one's courage reversed." One wounded parent told me that when his son was arrested by the police the experience was like having the wind knocked out of him. Another, when she discovered that her daughter was engaging in premarital sex, described her feeling as a deep sense of disappointment, wherein her hopes, desires, and expectations for her daughter were totally frustrated.

Instead of continuing to sink into discouragement or disappointment, these parents were blessed with the will to overcome their sense of despair over the actions of their children. The fact that you are reading this book and have read this far means that you, too, have the will to work to overcome parental discouragement.

The Search for Healing

Most wounded parents want answers for questions such as, "How did this happen? We did the best we could as parents, so what went wrong? Why did God allow this to happen? Why didn't God keep this from happening?" In reality, wounded parents do not need answers to such questions, if in fact there are answers. This information would not be helpful with regard to the future.

If you did have all the information as to why your child went astray, what would you do? Avoid a repeat performance with the next child? Possibly, but given the uniqueness of every child, it is not likely that information would make that much difference. Wounded parents do not need information as much as they need healing.

What do I mean by healing? First of all, we need to understand the nature of the wounds. The wounded parent's injuries are emotional: discouragement, disappointment, depression, despair, a sense of failure, anger, frustration, grief, guilt, a feeling of rejection, and self-pity. You recall we discussed these in chapter 4.

How is a physical wound treated? A diagnosis is made: location, size, type (for example, knife or bullet), depth, and the extent of damage. The wound is usually cleaned with antiseptic. If it is large, it may need stitches, then proper bandaging. Finally, time and considerable dependence on the body's restorative powers complete the process.

Emotional wounds need to be assessed also. This means that you begin with yourself: a deep, serious, and honest self-examination. This is a good biblical idea, as Paul once suggested (see I Cor. 11:28, 31). Many of us have never taken the time to look at ourselves closely. Examine, judge, discern, and evaluate the nature of your hurting. Whether it is self-pity, guilt, anger, or an honest anxiety for the welfare of the wayward son or daughter, at least *identify* the nature of the wound. How do you do this? I suggest two methods. Primarily you need to talk about your feelings so you can get a clear and objective look at them. This means you need to find one or more sets of willing-to-listen ears that will be understanding, objective, accepting, supportive, and reflective. In addition, you can determine to use this experience as an opportunity for your own spiritual growth. Therefore, I am suggesting both an individual and a group-oriented approach to healing. This is a program of working on yourself both in private and in a supportive group.

You may need to begin with individual counseling, if you have access to a qualified person. Consider your pastor: does he have the training and experience to help you? Some pastors do and others do not. At least consider the possibility of giving him the opportunity to help you. If he is not a good choice for counseling, there may be other possibilities: another pastor who is qualified by training and experience; a full-time clinical pastoral counselor in a counseling center; or a Christian professional counselor (psychologist, social worker, psychiatrist, or marriage and family counselor).

Moreover, you can find another wounded parent who has experienced healing from God. In your church, there are probably several. Such a person might be willing to be your sounding board. Remember that he or she has walked where you now walk and has something to offer you out of that experience. Such a search for experienced ears may well result in the discovery of a group of wounded parents.

The most important method of identifying your wounds and beginning the healing process will be your personal examination (although not entirely separate from your spouse). The examination I have in mind will seek to answer basic questions such as, "Who am I? What motivates my behavior? How do I feel about myself? What are my life goals? What kind of person am I? How do other people see me? How do I relate to those about me? In all honesty, what basic changes could I make in my attitudes and behavior that would improve the atmosphere in my home and the relationships I have with those nearest to me?"

The Birth of Hope

If you can discover some answers to the questions just listed, you will be on your way to change and growth. You will begin to experience the birth of hope. You may not be able to do much to change the attitudes and behavior of a rebellious son or daughter (at least it seems that way for the present), but you can do something about yourself.

When you get to the point where you can say, "I cannot change either the circumstances that surround my family and me or the course of events that have already transpired, but I can change *me*," then hope will have been born in your life. Please realize that I am not leaving God out in saying this. Actually, any deep desire on your part to change yourself will itself be a gift from God. God is not the God of stagnation.

How do you change yourself? You change by growing. But in this you are not alone. Growth is an act of God, because God is the creator of the life you have, and a vital part of that creative process is the process of growth. Your responsibility is to put yourself in a position where growth can be stimulated and encouraged.

When Harold and Connie Morris realized that Melissa might run away again at any time, they agreed that something had to change. Since they were virtually powerless to change Melissa, it occurred to them in counseling with their pastor that they could possibly do something about themselves. After all, why would Melissa want to run away from them? Why would she reject them? What were her peers offering her that her parents were not providing? Both Harold and Connie agreed with their pastor that they needed a serious re-examination of family priorities.

For the Morrises, their re-examination began with each of them as a parent. They decided to spend thirty minutes each morning in private, Harold in their bedroom and Connie in the kitchen before breakfast, in a systematic plan of

Bible reading and prayer, seeking specific ways to change themselves. Starting this simple endeavor brought a birth of hope into this family. This is not all they did or all that happened to them. I'm only pointing out how they started the process of growth in overcoming their parental discouragement.

Spiritual Growth: A New Strategy

What is spiritual growth? A clear definition is needed. There is a lot of confusion and narrow thinking about what these words mean. As I see it, spiritual growth is a process of developing one's relationship with God, who is revealed in Jesus Christ, and allowing God (with your active cooperation) to produce in you the personality and character He intended, which will reflect through your personal uniqueness something of the likeness of Jesus Christ. As a process, growth takes time. As long as there is life growth is taking place. Consequently, we never "arrive." The Christian is always in the process of *becoming*. The Christian life is a journey. Christians are pilgrims, not settlers. Recall that the basic invitation of Jesus to become one of His disciples was, "Follow me!" (John 21:22).

It is certainly possible for one's relationship to God to become stagnant, retarded, or arrested. I know. The sad thing about it was that for so long I was not aware of it. It took a crisis to expose my lack of growth. Many of us think that because we go to church regularly, participate in various church activities, hold certain offices in the church (even be the pastor!), have some familiarity with the Bible, and know how to offer a prayer, that we are spiritually mature. Such reasoning is shallow thinking.

Spiritual growth is a process in which one's relationship with God is maturing. The maturing process involves the several facets of one's total being: body, mind, spirit, life (or soul), and will. It includes becoming increasingly sensitive to the reality of the presence of God in my life. It includes expanding my awareness of God's plan and will for my life, including both the overall blueprint and the particular and daily details. It involves becoming increasingly responsive to the will of God for my life in both trust and obedience. The maturing process, in other words, involves a sensitizing of the inner person (see Eph. 3:16) to the presence and will of Jesus Christ in and for my life *and* for my family.

Moreover, spiritual growth is a process in which one's various social roles also mature. As a human being, you live out several roles in relation to others: husband or wife, father or mother, son or daughter, friend, neighbor, work associate, employer or employee, citizen, church member, member of a racial group, member of a profession or vocation (businessman or woman, pastor, mayor, senator, schoolteacher, principal, soldier, store manager, physician, attorney), aunt or uncle, nephew or niece. The list seems endless for each person. You see, as a human being you are not an isolated individual. You are a social being related in some way or another to other social beings. A maturing Christian life includes the way we live out *all* of these social roles. I cannot be a Christian *person* devoid of my responsibilities as a Christian *parent*. One automatically entails the other.

Therefore, the maturing process involves a sensitizing of the way I relate to others through all of my social roles as a follower of Jesus Christ. Love for God, for example, requires an effort to love others also (see I John 4:7–21). This is one reason why spiritual growth is so vital for improving our relationships with other people, including parent-child relationships.

Consequently, spiritual growth becomes a new strategy for overcoming parental discouragement. This was true for me and for several other wounded parents with whom I have worked. However, keep in mind that although wounded parents may feel driven to new experiences in spiritual growth because of their problems with their children, all of us have discovered that God was simply using (although not causing) our tragedies to bring us to a new and more mean-ingful relationship with Him, which helped us to become stronger Christian parents and persons than we had been.

Spiritual Growth: A Healing Process

In every instance, the wounded parents mentioned thus far discovered that spiritual growth, in time, was also a heal-ing process. When Phil and Constance Fisher discovered Jeff's involvement with drugs, they were thoroughly confused as to why Jeff would do such a thing. They could not under-stand why the influence of their Christian home had not served as a better deterrent than it had. They truly felt that they had done the best they could to provide Jeff with the environment of a God-centered, Christ-honoring home. They not only were disappointed in Jeff; they also were shaken about their Christian faith as they had understood and prac-ticed it. They felt that something vital must have been miss-ing. Their hurt was aimed not only at Jeff, but also toward their relationship with God.

When the Fishers reached the bottom of despair, they refused to acknowledge defeat as Christians. Instead, they determined to find out what was possibly missing in their relationship to God. Later, they decided that it wasn't any missing element in their Christian home that caused Jeff to do what he did. Several factors played a part in his choices. But the Fishers did discover a vital relationship with God as they chose to engage in a definite program of spiritual growth. As a by-product, spiritual growth became for them as wounded parents a healing process.

Specifically, what did the Fishers do? First of all, they both decided that as a result of their experience with Jeff they *wanted* to grow spiritually. Phil and Constance both believed that they could not afford to let this experience go by and not come out of it as stronger Christians, parents, and persons than they had been. Second, they committed themselves to a special private worship time with God each morning. A systematic program of Bible reading was chosen, along with prayer, meditation, and diary-keeping for recording prayer requests, impressions, and insights gained during this time.[1] The initial fifteen-minute time block gradually grew to thirty or more minutes.

Third, the Fishers began a program of reading carefully selected books by Christian writers. Several good suggestions came from their minister, the church librarian, and a local Christian bookstore manager. From time to time, Phil and Constance would discuss with each other what they were learning from their reading. They found that by reserving an hour for such reading before retiring to bed, they could read several books a year.

Fourth, the Fishers sought out other wounded parents, and with the help of their minister began meeting with three other couples on a regular basis in the homes of the group members. For two hours, one evening a week for several weeks, these couples shared their common struggles, offering each other insight, support, and encouragement. The Fishers discovered that by combining their private spiritual growth disciplines with a sharing-group experience, they not only received considerable stimulus for growth but also contributed to the growth of other parents who had been through similar experiences.

After several months, the Fishers realized that a healing process had been taking place in their lives and that their feelings of discouragement had turned into an exciting adventure of discovering levels of living never known before. This is not to imply that all of Jeff's problems evaporated. Phil and Constance continued to go through some difficult times with their son. However, it wasn't long before Jeff realized that something unusual was happening to his par-

1. A suggested resource is Peter Lord, *The 2959 Plan: A Guide to Communion with God* (Grand Rapids: Baker, 1980).

ents, and the changes taking place in their lives, in time, became the stimulus for change in Jeff's behavior and attitudes.

Spiritual Growth: A New Goal

The Fishers discovered a new goal for their family: spiritual growth. This is not to suggest that spiritual growth should become an end in itself. Quite the contrary. The Fishers' growth became the means for God to become a vital life-changing force in their lives. Instead of being consumed by self-pity, discouragement, anger, depression, and despair, Phil and Constance released Jeff to God's care and did something about themselves.

As their relationship with God deepened, the Fishers learned that Jeff was not simply *their* problem. He was God's problem, too; and God had His own special way of dealing with Jeff. They learned to release Jeff into God's keeping each morning. This was a tremendous relief. Spiritual growth brought an awareness of God's control of their unique situation.

By concentrating daily on the nature and depth of our relationship with God, we are less likely to become sidetracked by anxiety, worry, and fear over what's happening or could happen to our children. Moreover, healthy spiritual growth (not the egocentric, "Jesus and I," self-absorbed kind) motivates us to reach out to others who are experiencing similar problems and pain and offer our healing support.

The God who turned a cross into a resurrection can work similar wonders in your family, although maybe not in the way you desire or expect. In a few years hence you can look back and see that God knew what He was doing and did the best thing for everyone involved.

The Strength of a Support Group

Wounded parents tend to feel cut off and alone in their dilemma. It is normal to want to withdraw from others when your son or daughter behaves in a way that you feel reflects badly on your parenting and Christian faith. You are embarrassed. You feel like a failure. You don't know what to say when people ask what happened or how it happened. This is doubly difficult if you are a respected leader in a church. Imagine how a pastor feels when he recalls the words of I Timothy 3:5, "for if a man does not know to manage his own household, how can he care for God's church?" It doesn't help much to remember that "the sons of Eli [the priest] were worthless men; they had no regard for the LORD" (I Sam. 2:12), or that Samuel's sons went astray (I Sam. 8:3).

This is the time when you need other people, especially those who have walked where you walk and have strength to offer. My experience with wounded parents has taught me that involvement in a small support group is invaluable. You will learn that you are not alone. Most every church has several wounded parents. Ask your pastor to help you arrange for a group to meet together to discuss the possibility of becoming a supporting ministry to each other. Several books about small groups could be consulted for getting started. See Appendix B, "Books about Small Groups," for a list of suggested titles.

A support group can offer a sounding board for your feelings, helping you to understand them. A support group can give you a sense of a larger family of concern. The typical nuclear family (father, mother, children) lives at a great distance from other relatives, for example, grandparents, aunts, uncles, or cousins. This extended family once functioned to provide considerable support and encouragement during times of crisis. A support group can help to make up for that loss. A support group can offer the knowledge of wider experience, helpful suggestions, ideas for coping, and evaluations of your opinions that could prove beneficial as you try to relate to a wayward child.

A support group can in several ways become a type of life-support system for an unstable family situation, without which that family would disintegrate. Remember the discussion in chapter 3—a wayward son or daughter can create a strain on the marriage of the parents.

Specific suggestions for creating a support group will be mentioned in chapter 10.

The Pain and the Gain of Growth

At first, spiritual growth can be painful. Many active church people have great difficulty admitting to themselves or to others that they need to change. They mistakenly believe that after twenty, thirty, or forty years in the church they have "arrived," that they represent the epitome of what Christianity is about, that there is little if anything left to learn or discover. Why is this? Pride is the answer for some. They prefer to live in the illusion that theirs is normal Christianity. The answer for others is that they truly believe that they have done all that is expected of them, that there is nothing else to learn, and that God has revealed in their experiences everything He has to offer.

It is not easy to look at your spouse and say, "I have made more than my share of mistakes; this crisis in our home is driving me to my knees to pray as I've never prayed before; I am not the Christian I ought to be; my relationship to God is cool and distant (or, I'm confused about why God allowed this to happen); and I am going to do something about it. Will you join me?" For some, it will be the most difficult thing they have ever done.

Moreover, the thought of exposing your fears, failures, frustrations, and doubts, even to a group of fellow Christians you can trust and who truly love and accept you, can be intimidating to some people. Actually to do so, at first, can be painful. The pain is real. But the gain makes it worthwhile.

The pain of humiliation, confession, and repentance is replaced by the gain of growth: strength, forgiveness, joy, discovery, encouragement, renewal, reconciliation, not to speak of the new adventures in living that God will open to you. If you want to overcome your parental discouragement, you will have to get involved in the rigors and discipline of spiritual growth. Your wayward son or daughter may not come back as did the prodigal son (Luke 15:11–32) in the way or the time you desire, but a new beginning will have begun *in you.* And that's a start worth starting!

Questions for Discussion

1. What word describes your present feeling toward your wayward son or daughter?
2. Do you identify with the idea of a need for healing? If so, what is the nature of your emotional wounds?
3. What basic changes can you make in your attitudes and behavior that would improve the atmosphere in your home?
4. What does the phrase *spiritual growth* mean to you? Are you presently experiencing any? Describe this growth.
5. How can spiritual growth be a healing process?

8

Building a
New Relationship

A wounded parent can neither correct all the mistakes of the past nor bring a son or daughter back to the relationship that existed five or ten years earlier. Present realities must be squarely faced and accepted. Although you may not agree with your child's lifestyle, values, or behavior, it will help the family situation greatly if you can merely accept the fact that "this is the way it is." Such acceptance will facilitate immensely your next move: trying to build a new relationship. This will not always be easy, nor can it be done quickly, but you can start in this direction.

From Parents to Friends

All parents should be working themselves out of the job of being parents and easing themselves into the relationship of being friends of their children. This is especially true of wounded parents. I am not suggesting that you cannot be both parents and friends at the same time during the early formative years of your children's lives. By the phrase *the job of being parents*, I mean the role of parenting. But as children grow up, the role of parenting by father and mother should diminish while the role of friend should increase.

The application of this point obviously depends on the age of your son or daughter. A thirteen-year-old daughter certainly is in greater need of parental direction than a twenty-one-year-old. But the process of shifting from predominantly parent to predominantly friend is an ongoing one. You will have to be the judge of the degree of parental control and direction currently needed.

Yet, let's face reality. If your son or daughter has largely rejected you and what you stand for morally and spiritually, you have already lost control and probably cannot regain it. Control can be exercised effectively only as long as there is a basic respect for you as her or his parent. If respect has gone, so has control.

Some readers may object to the word *control*. I don't care for it myself, but essentially I am referring to direction, influence, discipline, veto power over certain decisions, and guidance. What this means in specific instances depends on several variables. A three-year-old boy who heads out to cross a busy street alone needs one kind of control. A sixteen-year-old boy who insists on your buying him an automobile needs another. There isn't much you can do to stop older teen-agers, and certainly young adults, from experimenting with drugs, sex, or alternative religious lifestyles if they are headstrong and determined to do it.

My point is this: regardless of the age of your child and the circumstances of the present ruptured relationship, you would be wise to minimize the parenting and maximize the friendship. The older the child is, the more advisable this becomes. For whatever reasons, he or she resents your parenting. It will be difficult for him or her to resent your friendship. He or she does not want to be controlled, but understood and accepted as a person.

When I first offered this advice to Kay and Steve Wonder after they had several explosive confrontations with their son Marshall, who was involved in the college drug scene, Kay replied, "But I'm his *mother*; in *no way* can I be anything else." It took several months for Kay to accept the fact that Marshall deeply resented her *smothering* control. When Kay began to shift to being an understanding friend, the Wonders were able to build a new relationship with their son.

From Being Judgmental to Being Respectful

In building a new relationship, wounded parents need to stop being judgmental and to try being respectful of their children. Not all wounded parents have been judgmental, to be sure, but most of the ones I have counseled have been and continue to be until they realize that a judgmental attitude blocks any future reconciliation.

Parenting tends to be heavy on oughts and ought nots, shoulds and should nots, and rightly so in communicating moral boundaries to developing children. But through the years, this process needs to diminish while a developing dialogue pertaining to morality and religious faith should increase between parent and child.

A major problem I have noticed in the parenting process is that some parents maintain a heavy emphasis on oughts and ought nots and expand this role to condemnation for misbehavior with little concern for why the child is misbehaving. To continue being judgmental toward your wayward son or daughter will only make matters worse. Your children already know you disapprove of certain types of behavior. A negative, judgmental attitude only widens the gap.

What is needed is respect. To respect someone means that you feel or show esteem for and honor that person. If you respect someone you show consideration and regard for and avoid violation of that person. This includes expressions of appreciation and deference. To esteem means to regard as of a high order, and to prize.

When I suggested this to one wounded parent, he replied, "But he [his son] doesn't deserve my respect after what he has done." That is to miss the point of respect, as well as the value of human beings from a Christian perspective. Respect is not something to be earned or deserved. It is given. Children, whatever their age, are inherently valuable and to be prized. This is a clear teaching of the Bible (Pss. 127:3–5; 128:3–4; Mark 10:13–16).

There is a tendency among adults to think of respect as that which children should show their parents, when it is equally important for parents to show respect for their children. Where prodigal children have poor self-images, there tends to have been little respect shown to them by their parents. The person with a positive self-image tends to be the one whose parents esteemed him or her through the formative years.

To respect your son or daughter means that you stop judging and condemning and start nurturing. Nurturing calls for understanding, caring, and encouraging (as you are allowed to). I am not referring to a smothering kind of protection. This would violate that sense of independence your son or daughter is striving for. There is no simple "how to do it" formula for nurturing a wayward child. It will be expressed more in your attitude than in your words.

This attitude of respect communicates the message, "I may not agree with what you have done or the way you are living, but I do not condemn you; I regard you as a person of infinite worth; I am with you as a friend; I will assist whenever I am needed and where such assistance is acceptable; I encourage you to find the fullness of life's meaning; I offer you my trust, love, and appreciation."

From Talking to Listening

The process of building a new relationship with your child will show a quality of respect that moves from a stance of talking to one of listening. If you can stop being heavy on advice-giving and start trying to understand how that son or daughter truly feels, you will have made significant progress. Most wounded parents talk too much. This is another expression of the "heavy parent" role (the controlling parent).

There is also a "healthy parent" role, referred to as nurturing, and a part of nurturing is listening. When Karen Johnston began to listen to Robby, she discovered a boy who was deeply resentful over his father leaving them and who was subconsciously blaming his mother for driving his father away.

When Art and Betty Collins started listening to Irene, they found a lonely girl who felt unloved and unwanted. She had sought love and acceptance in her basically unhappy high-school peer group, but their abuse of alcohol became her retreat from unhappiness.

When Jack and Robin Stevens began listening to Richard, they found a discouraged young man who was made to feel that he would never be able to measure up to Ronald and Roger Marks, the brothers next door. Richard felt he could never please his parents by being himself. Ronald and Roger got more of Richard's parents' attention than he could. Therefore, he reasoned, "If I'm no good as I am, then I might as well prove it." So he drove his car recklessly, getting into trouble with the police. This brought about his parents' attention, even if in a negative way.

If you will listen carefully to your children, you will learn a great deal about yourself. You may not like what you learn, but listening is an essential ingredient in building a new relationship.

On Turning Loose

Some wounded parents I have known have unwittingly made matters worse with their son or daughter by trying to hang on to the parental reins and continue controlling things, even when it is obviously futile. To build a new relationship, it is much better to *turn loose* of the parental controls.

When Susan Wallace realized that her parents eventually had decided no longer to try to control her life, she was open to communicating with them. When J. C. and Phyllis Harper stopped trying to choose Buffy's friends for him, stopped nagging him to go to church, and stopped overloading him with all kinds of advice about how to behave, the atmosphere in the home began to change. J. C. quietly but firmly told Buffy that if at age sixteen he wanted to run the serious risk in the local school drug scene, be arrested, and face juvenile-court action and possible detention, then he would have to be prepared to pay the price. J. C. added that he and Phyllis had asked God for direction and that it seemed best to turn loose of the entire situation. They were not going to fret, plead, or be anxious about it anymore. They would have to make this decision afresh each morning, but they were going to turn loose and let God take charge. The responsibility for his behavior was placed firmly on Buffy. This was the beginning of this boy's sober reversal of behavior.

Turning loose seems, among other things, to remove one side of the conflict and give God room to work.

On Trusting God

The other, and more vital, side of turning loose is to trust God to take your family situation into His hands and begin to work redemptively. After all, when you've done all you can do and it doesn't work or nothing happens for the better, doesn't it make sense to let God take charge of the ruptured relationship between you and your child?

Several wounded couples have told me that they were unable to have any peace about their wayward children until they learned to pray the prayer of relinquishment. This is not merely a one-time prayer, but a way of praying daily until God has an opportunity to reverse the situation.

One parent expressed the nature of such prayer:

O God, I love my son very much. I tried to be a good father, as best I knew how, to him, although I'm sure I made plenty of mistakes. I don't fully understand why he has turned out the way he has. He has no room for You in his life. His actions lately I deplore. But I do not know what else to do. His mother and I are at the end of the road and we are brokenhearted. *We turn loose of our son today and place him into Your hands.* We give him to You as You once gave him to us. We believe You love him, infinitely more than we do. We ask that You take complete charge of this entire situation. We ask for Your will to be done in all of our lives. Show his mother and me what changes we need to make in our relationship to him. Thank You for Your love which gives us hope. Amen.

Getting out of the way and simply trusting God to bring about the necessary changes are extremely difficult things for wounded parents to do, but God works so much better and more quickly when we are not interfering with His efforts. Moreover, God has chosen to work through the faith (trust) of His people, even the faith of wounded parents. To paraphrase Psalm 127:1, "Unless the Lord builds this new parent-child relationship, those who build it labor in vain."

Moreover, turning loose is not rejecting your child. It is placing him or her totally in God's hands. It is availing yourself of God's resources for dealing with what, humanly speaking, is an impossible situation.

Recognizing Your Child's Rights

For years, you have had hopes and dreams for your son or daughter. Yet because of what has happened, these have been largely shattered. If you are going to see a new relationship between you develop, then it is important that you recognize your child's right to choose his or her own lifestyle.

Where there is no freedom to choose, there can be little or no meaningful relating as friends. Naturally, freedom involves risk. But recognize that when God created the human race, He ran the same risk you and I ran when we chose to bring children into the world. There were no guarantees. God expects us to be willing to run the same risks He ran when He made all of us.

My son has the right to be what he wants and chooses to be (as long as that choice does not cause harm to other people). Your daughter has the right to become what she chooses. We may not like or agree with their choices. But they deserve the same freedom we had when we were their age.

As long as we parents insist on placing certain arbitrary restrictions on our children's choices, it will be difficult for them to relate freely and enjoyably to us. In many instances parental restrictions and conditions force some children, seeking their self-identity and independence, to choose alternative lifestyles, including both moral and spiritual behavior patterns. Call it stubborn rebellion, bullheadedness, or obstinancy if you will, but some youth, when given no choice, will prove their independence by going the opposite direction from their parents' choices.

I am not talking about house rules, regulations for using the car, and other day-to-day family expectations for cooperative and responsible living that are usually needed for preteens and teen-agers. I am talking about life goals, moral and religious commitments that affect one's entire life, and cultural and spiritual lifestyles, along with their behavioral expressions. I am talking about youth's basic questions, such as, "What kind of person will I be? Whom will I choose to relate to on deep and meaningful levels? What is really important in life? What in life has ultimate value? What is the meaning of morality and spirituality?"

Our children have the right to answer those questions for themselves. We will certainly influence their answers by both words and example, but the final decision is theirs. When they know we recognize their freedom to choose, and we respect their freedom even to choose differently than we do, it will go a long way to build a new relationship when we have our differences and disagreements as parents and children. If they are not free to violate our moral code and reject our religious beliefs, then they are not truly free even to behave morally and believe religiously as we do.

However, your children's rights end where others' and society's begin. They need to clearly understand that if they choose to break the law or disrupt the stability of the family they will have to be prepared to suffer the consequences. You do not really help your children when you protect them from the consequences of such behavior. In recent years, some wounded parents are discovering that it pays off when parental love "gets tough," holds the line on family rules with penalties for violations, even allows a child to discover what it's like to go to jail, organizes parent groups to assist each other in combating peer pressure and a hostile youth subculture, and practices firm discipline. In other words, they have learned that simple understanding and forgiveness without firm discipline do not work.[1]

Your Child's Need for Your Faith

If you want to build a new relationship with your son or daughter, he or she needs not only the freedom to be him or her self but also your faith in him or her. There is no stimulus like that of the confidence which one person, especially a significant other, expresses toward another. (A significant other is a person whose influence and approval are important to another person.)

I have often heard the wayward children of wounded parents say, "My parents don't think I can do anything right. They don't care what happens to me. No one believes in me." Consequently, these children tend to be discouraged. Rudolf Dreikurs, the famous child psychiatrist, contended

1. See the story about Toughlove, an association of parents who draw the line against out-of-control youngsters and force them to behave or leave home, in "Getting Tough with Teens," *Time*, June 8, 1981, p. 47.

that misbehaving children are discouraged children.[2] The opposite should also be true: encouraged children tend to be cooperative. Self-confidence is often the result of someone having confidence in you.

The faith of significant others is a stimulating and motivating power in one's life. There is a strong inclination in human beings to live up to the expectations of parents. If you can shift your expectations from the negative, based on past misbehavior, to the positive, based on "the assurance of things hoped for" (Heb. 11:1), you will begin to experience a new relationship with your child. Faith solicits faith. Hope solicits hope. Confidence (from you) will solicit confidence (on the part of your child). People tend to want to carry on a good relationship with those who believe in them, and this applies to children as well.

Keep the Lines of Communication Open

To build a new relationship with your child, you will need to take the initiative in keeping the lines of communication open. This calls for unconditional openness. If you take the attitude, "I don't want to talk with you unless you . . . ," then don't expect any communication to take place.

You don't have to compromise your moral convictions or religious beliefs in order to be open in communication. If your son or daughter has moved out of the house or lives at a distance due to location of a job, you can still call or write, but keep the conversation or subject on a nonjudgmental level. He or she knows how you feel about value differences between you. Your son or daughter wants to know if you still care, in spite of differences. Is a communicating friendship still possible? You will have to decide.

Obviously, in some cases, your child simply may not want to communicate with you at present. There's too much anger

2. Rudolf Dreikurs and Vicki Soltz, *Children: The Challenge* (New York: Hawthorn Books, 1964), chapter 3.

being felt now. If so, wait for a while and be available and responsive when he or she does call or write.

In the meantime, as you have opportunity, be ready to be more of a friend than a controlling parent, to be more respectful than judgmental, to listen more than to talk, to turn loose and trust the situation to God, to respect your child's right to make his or her own decisions yet to be firm in your love as you hold the line on your family rules, to believe in your child as a person of worth, and to keep the lines of communication open. A new relationship may develop between you, although this will always take time and patience.

Questions for Discussion

1. How do you feel about shifting from the role of parent to that of friend with your children?
2. Are you engaging in any kind of smothering control of your children?
3. What does it mean to be judgmental of your children? respectful?
4. What does it mean to nurture and to listen at home? to express faith in each other?
5. How do you turn loose and trust God with respect to your children?
6. Does your child have any rights?
7. To what extent should you protect your child from the consequences of his or her behavior?

9

Building a New Self-image

As you, a wounded parent, attempt to build a new relationship with your rebellious child, it is also important for you not to neglect yourself. The self-image of a wounded parent is not likely to be in good shape. It probably bears the trappings of failure and defeat. A battered self-image needs to be repaired. Yours may even need a transplant!

Some people who have undergone plastic surgery suddenly developed what seemed to be a new self-image. Believing in their new attractiveness and beauty, they began accepting and even loving themselves in a healthy way. You may not need plastic surgery in order to develop a new self-image. God has His own unique methods of the spirit.

The Shattered Self-image

When Christian, church-going parents lose a son or daughter to a non-Christian, secular, and immoral culture, it does something to them. They tend to conclude that something is wrong with them, their family, their home life, and even the quality of their Christian faith.

To experience what seems to be failure as a parent shatters one's self-image. By self-image, I mean the way you see yourself and the way you feel about yourself. Feelings of worthlessness, inferiority, loneliness, and inadequacy often overwhelm a wounded parent. You want to withdraw from people, especially those who thought you were an exemplary Christian parent. Now that they know "the ugly truth," you don't want to face them. You feel that you are a handicapped, second-class Christian. Other parents may be OK, but you have concluded, "I'm not OK."[1]

If there are other children at home, you may tend to become fearful that they will be like the one that went astray. Such fear could cause you either to become overprotective of those others or afraid to discipline them for fear that they will rebel also. Parental paralysis can easily set in. The basic problem is not what the other children do or don't do, but how you feel about yourself.

A shattered self-image needs treatment: a good dose of self-respect, self-acceptance, and self-love. This is the time to be a good parent to yourself: stop kicking yourself, stop putting yourself down, stop scolding yourself, stop calling yourself names ("stupid," "dummy," "no-good," "failure," "bad"). Treat yourself as a good parent would.[2] To put it another way, how would a close friend treat you at this time? Treat yourself that way. You will make a serious mistake if you go on breaking your shattered self-image into smaller pieces.

The Creative Possibilities of Disappointment

When you start to build a new self-image, it will be important for you to realize that God has more at stake in this process than you or anyone else does. The Bible makes

1. See Thomas A. Harris, *I'm OK, You're OK: A Practical Guide to Trans-actional Analysis* (New York: Harper and Row, 1969), pp. 43–46, for a clinical discussion of this idea.

2. W. Hugh Missildine and Lawrence Galton, *Your Inner Conflicts: How to Solve Them* (New York: Simon and Schuster, 1974), pp. 15ff.

it clear in the beginning that you were created in the image of God (Gen. 1:27). A sense of failure causes one to have poor inner vision and thus to have a distorted view of that image. God wants you to see yourself as you really are: in His image. From the perspective of the New Testament the original image of God was marred by sin, but through salvation in Jesus Christ, the Christian has put on (as one puts on clothes) a new nature, "which is being renewed in knowledge after the image of its creator" (Col. 3:10).

The old image (the one marred by sin) has been replaced by a new image (the new nature in Christ). As Paul says, "Just as we have borne the image of the man of dust, we shall [or, let us] also bear the image of the man of heaven [Christ]" (I Cor. 15:49). The image God wants you to see in yourself is not a distorted view of yourself due to problems, defeats, and discouragements experienced in the human parenting process. The image in you is not contingent on your achievements and efforts as a parent. It is a given: the image of God after the likeness of Jesus Christ.

Actually, God is able to use your experiences in life to re-create His image in you. Notice Romans 8:28–30: "We know that in everything God works for good with those who love him, who are called according to his purpose. For those whom he foreknew he also predestined to be conformed to the image of his Son, in order that he might be the firstborn [the preeminent one] among many brethren. And those whom he predestined he also called; and those whom he called he also justified; and those whom he justified he also glorified." These verses say that God is shaping His people into the image of His Son. This is the "good" that God "works for" in using "everything" in our experiences, including what happens to us as parents.

This idea is also supported in II Corinthians 3:18, "And we all, with unveiled face, beholding the glory of the Lord, are being changed into his likeness [image] from one degree of glory to another; for this comes from the Lord who is the

Spirit." In Galatians 4:19, Paul wrote to the Galatian Christians that he was feeling great concern for them, even pains like those of childbirth, "until Christ be formed" in them. In the midst of our apparent parental failures, God is changing us into the likeness or image of His Son who is being formed in us. To build a new self-image means to recognize the new image of God in Christ which God is forming at the very core of your personality.

These truths should make wounded Christian parents confident that creative possibilities exist even in disappointments in childrearing. God wants you to see not your distorted image of defeat but Christ's new image of victory. What kind of person you are is not dependent on what you did or did not do but on what Christ has done *for* you in the past (on the cross) and is doing *in* you in the present.

By the grace and help of God you can turn your failures and disappointments into positive forces. I like the way Robert Schuller redefines the meaning of failure:

> *Failure doesn't mean* you are a failure. . . . *It does mean* you haven't succeeded yet.
>
> *Failure doesn't mean* you have accomplished nothing. . . . *It does mean* you have learned something.
>
> *Failure doesn't mean* you have been a fool. . . . *It does mean* you had a lot of faith.
>
> *Failure doesn't mean* you've been disgraced. . . . *It does mean* you were willing to try.
>
> *Failure doesn't mean* you don't have it. . . . *It does mean* you have to do something in a different way.
>
> *Failure doesn't mean* you are inferior. . . . *It does mean* you are not perfect.
>
> *Failure doesn't mean* you've wasted your life. . . . *It does mean* you have a reason to start afresh.
>
> *Failure doesn't mean* you should give up. . . . *It does mean* you must try harder.
>
> *Failure doesn't mean* you'll never make it. . . . *It does mean* it will take a little longer.

Failure doesn't mean God has abandoned you. . . . *It does mean* God has a better idea![3]

In the hands of God, the creative possibilities of disappointment as a parent are limitless. There is too much at stake in your family for you to call it quits and retreat into the losers' retirement home. God is still in the process of making a new person out of you by using the experiences you are having with your children. Moreover, your children are watching how you respond to this difficult situation. Wounded parents would be wise to affirm each morning Schuller's now-famous possibility-thinker's creed:

> When faced with a mountain
> I will not quit.
> I will keep on striving
> until I
> climb over,
> find a pass through,
> tunnel underneath,
> or simply stay and
> turn the mountain
> into a gold mine!
> With God's help![4]

A New Search for Security

Many wounded parents reason that if they do the best they can to rear their children in a Christian home and in the life of the church, and these children (or at least one of them) still go astray morally and spiritually, then family life in particular and life in general is insecure. Anything can happen to wipe out your hopes and dreams. Such reasoning produces a rather shaky feeling of uncertainty. Is God not always fully in control?

3. Robert H. Schuller, *You Can Become the Person You Want to Be* (New York: Hawthorn Books, 1973), p. 73.
4. *Ibid.*, p. 28.

Of course God is in control. He has not abandoned His creation or deserted His people. However, we are not God's robots. He gives each of us the freedom to make our own decisions, and He respects our freedom. We could not be persons in the fullest sense without freedom to choose. The prodigal son was free to go off into a far country and squander his inheritance in loose living (Luke 15:11–19). However, notice that he was not free to avoid suffering the consequences (go hungry, feed swine for a living, and regret his decisions). Freedom is not absolutely unlimited.

It is risky being a parent. It is risky being a son or daughter. Life is full of risks. Life with no risks would be not only a fantasy but also a dull existence. But does this imply that there can be no security? Of course not.

Parents can find security, but not *outside* of themselves; money, status, position, possessions, prestige, friends, health—anyone or anything can be taken away from you or lost. Security must come from *within*: who you are in a personal relationship with God. As a child of God through faith in Jesus Christ, you have all the security you need to face whatever life brings. That kind of security contributes to a strong and positive self-image.

If, as a wounded parent, you will examine carefully who you are in a personal relationship with God, you will be on track in finding a sense of security that will strengthen your self-image. This in turn will improve your relationship with those in your family. Insecure people are usually not easy to get along with. Secure people tend to have the strength to love even the unlovable.

Loving Yourself into a New Self-image

If your children have not turned out as you had hoped they would, you may be blaming yourself to the point of self-depreciation, even self-hate. Punishing yourself for "all of those mistakes I made" simply adds to a poor self-image. But if you want to build a new self-image, then face reality and do something about it. If you honestly feel you made certain mistakes in rearing your children, then admit those mistakes to your children, to your mate, and to yourself. Ask their forgiveness and God's. Most likely your biggest problem will be yourself. Can you forgive yourself?

Being a good parent to yourself means loving yourself, respecting yourself as a person made in God's image, and accepting yourself as an imperfect human being. Jesus taught that the two great commandments in the Bible are love for God and love for one's neighbor. Notice how the second commandment is stated: "You shall love your neighbor *as yourself*" (Matt. 22:39, italics mine; cf. Lev. 19:18). Jesus assumed that a certain degree of self-love is normal, and, I would add, healthy. This is not an inordinate and egotistical self-love, but a healthy care, respect, and acceptance of one's self. If you cannot love yourself in that way, you probably will not be able to love others either.

There are no simple steps to follow in loving yourself into a new self-image. I suggest that you start with God's love for you if at this time you don't have the strength to love yourself. You can read some good books on this subject.[5] You can get involved with a group of Christian people who can teach you how to love yourself (see chapter 10 about support groups). You can secure professional counseling to help you deal realistically with the specifics of your difficulty in loving yourself.

The Tranquillity of a New Self-image

When you begin to feel good about yourself, you will be less tense, less irritable, and more at peace with yourself

5. See Cecil Osborne, *The Art of Learning to Love Yourself* (Grand Rapids: Zondervan, 1976); Robert H. Schuller, *Self-Love: The Dynamic Force of Success* (New York: Hawthorn Books, 1969); Walter Trobisch, *Self-acceptance and Depression* (Downers Grove, IL: Inter-Varsity, 1976); William A. Miller, *You Count—You Really Do!* (Minneapolis: Augsburg, 1977), especially part 2, "How to Improve Your Image of Yourself."

and with others than you were before. The tranquillity that comes with a new self-image will bring about an atmosphere in the home that will facilitate better communication and understanding among family members. When mother and father each have a positive self-regard, relationships in the home are relaxed and enjoyable.

At first your children may not understand what is going on. They may think that you've been drinking! When the shouting diminishes, the tension goes away, the frowning switches to smiling, and judging turns to nurturing, the children will be confused initially. But, believe me, they will enjoy it.

I am not trying to portray a utopia in suggesting that a new self-image on the part of parents will change everything. There will still be problems to solve and conflicts to resolve, but parents who have a strong, positive self-image, who like themselves, who have a warm, accepting self-regard, and who feel secure within will obviously create an atmosphere in the home where the members of the family will feel encouraged to act in a cooperative way toward each other.

There will still be rules to keep, responsibilities to perform, and moral expectations to support by parental example. Parents will still need to back up their word with firmness and consistency. Broken rules will bring certain consequences. But parents with positive self-images project an optimism that things are going to get better in the family, that the future is bright, and that a new day will bring new and better relationships. This kind of confidence is truly contagious.

Christ, the Best Model

Jesus Christ is our best model of a person with a strong, positive self-image. He knew who He was, why He was here, what His mission and purpose in life were, where He was going, and what life was all about. We find no evidence in the New Testament of Jesus depreciating Himself or despising Himself.

Jesus obviously liked Himself, enjoyed Himself, and had a positive and warm self-regard. He expressed a deep sense of inner security, knowing that His life was in the hands of His heavenly Father.

Although Jesus experienced disappointment in others, He never let that sink Him into depression. He stayed in control of His discouraging moments, turning them into opportunities for personal growth and for blessing other people.

Wounded parents can do no better than to get to know this Person revealed in the Gospels of the New Testament and let Him build, develop, or transplant this new self-image into their hearts and minds. You can know who you are, why you are here, where you are going, what your mission and purpose in life are, and what the purpose of life is. You can learn to like yourself, enjoy being you, and have a positive, warm self-regard. You can have a deep sense of inner security, knowing that your life is in the hands of God, your heavenly Father.

By the Power of God

All of this is possible by the power of God. He is able to bring this to pass. He who made you can remake you. A new you is possible by the power of God. You can't remake yourself, but God can.

If you are a wounded parent, you have experienced deep disappointment. You are in pain. You are hurting. Some of this may be self-inflicted by the kind of parenting you have done. But that is all past. You cannot go back and change that. You may be the victim of forces outside your home, and those forces are outside of your control. You are trying to get your emotions under control. You are trying to build a new relationship with your wayward son or daughter. You may now have begun to do something about yourself, to build a new self-image. But remember—any lasting change in you and in your child or children will have to be the work of God. It will be by His resources, intervention, and guidance that the relationship in your family will change for the better. So keep in close touch with Him and trust Him. He may not do things according to your plan, but He has more at stake in your family than you do, and He knows what He is doing.

Questions for Discussion

1. How would you describe your present self-image?
2. Can you identify some creative possibilities of disappointment in your family situation?
3. Can you see evidences of God making a new person out of you? Describe these evidences.
4. What are your reactions to the idea of self-love?
5. How can Jesus Christ be our model for a positive self-image?

10

Wounded Parents
Supporting Each Other

People with physical problems often find strength in sharing their common experiences. Cancer patients, people with heart ailments, and physically handicapped people who learn to use artificial limbs and wheelchairs have discovered unusual resources of encouragement in living and working together in a clinic or hospital. Wounded parents can likewise find considerable strength, wisdom, and encouragement by sharing their journey in a fellowship of struggle. They have a lot to offer each other.

You Are Not Alone

I trust that by the time you have read this far that you, as a wounded parent, are aware of an important fact: you are not alone. Probably there are more of you than you realize. Wounded parents have a tendency to keep their pain to themselves. It is not something they are eager or quick to share, especially in the fellowship of their church.

But let me assure you with double emphasis: you are not alone. In every church with which I have been familiar, I have found several, sometimes many, wounded parents who are depressed and discouraged about their relationship with one or more of their children. They do not know what to do about their particular situation. They often feel ashamed, embarrassed, or humiliated as they try to go on living a Christian life before others when one or more of their children did not choose to follow their example. Such parents often become dropouts from the church, either dropping out of leadership or teaching roles, or dropping out of church attendance altogether.

Wounded parents often reason that if they cannot influence their own children to live a Christian and active church life then how can they (or should they) try to influence other people's children? Therefore, they choose to withdraw from involvement in the church.

My response is this: the church is engaged in a major spiritual war in the midst of a hostile and secular battlefield, and the church is suffering many casualties. The injured need to and can help each other.

You are not alone. You are not weird, strange, or odd in your situation. Most Christian parents do not experience perfect bliss and conflict-free relations with their children. All Christian parents have problems; these problems simply vary in kind and degree of intensity. To be sure, some parents are more successful than others, but if you are hurting in some way because of the behavior and attitudes of one of your children, you are *not* abnormal.

There are several parents like you out there. You need each other. You can help each other. Why not find each other and do something about your situation *together*?

The Wounded Healer

Several years ago, Henri J. M. Nouwen, who was then teaching at Yale Divinity School, wrote *The Wounded Healer*. The title was suggested in an old legend Nouwen found in the Talmud, the collection of ancient rabbinic writings which make up the basis of religious authority for traditional Judaism. The legend is this:

> Rabbi Yoshua ben Levi came upon Elijah the prophet while he was standing at the entrance of Rabbi Simeron ben Yohai's cave. . . . He asked Elijah, "When will the Messiah come?"
>
> Elijah replied, "Go and ask him yourself."
>
> "Where is he?"
>
> "Sitting at the gates of the city."
>
> "How shall I know him?"
>
> "He is sitting among the poor covered with wounds. The others unbind all their wounds at the same time and then bind them up again. But he unbinds one at a time and binds it up again, saying to himself, 'Perhaps I shall be needed: if so I must always be ready so as not to delay for a moment.' "[1]

The story reveals that the Messiah is to be found among the poor, needy, and injured, binding His own wounds one at a time, anticipating the moment when His healing care will be needed. So it can be with wounded Christian parents who are growing spiritually through their experiences. They must look after their own wounds, but at the same time be ready to offer healing support to other wounded parents.

Your wounds of disappointment, heartache, and discouragement as a parent can be filled with purpose and meaning as you reach out to other wounded parents to heal their injured spirits.

Arthur and Betsy Wallace found several wounded parents in their new congregation. This pastor and his wife could quickly identify with these others and offer help, based on their own defeats and victories. Pretenses of religiosity were stripped away in an atmosphere of honesty and genuine caring, so much so that even wounded parents outside the con-

---

1. Henri J. M. Nouwen, *The Wounded Healer: Ministry in Contemporary Society* (Garden City, NY: Doubleday, 1972), pp. 83ff.

gregation gravitated toward the Wallaces for help. The model of ministry established by the Wallaces encouraged several of these parents to become wounded healers themselves.

Creating Support Groups

One beneficial way for wounded parents to help each other is through the opportunity offered in a support group. Before attempting to create a support group, it is important to understand something of small-group dynamics. Become familiar with the literature about small groups. See Appendix B, "Books about Small Groups," for a suggested list of books that can offer considerable help. Some or all of these may be found in nearby church, college, or city libraries.

The next step in creating a support group is to locate other wounded parents. You might ask your pastor to assist you. He probably has been counseling some. Keep your initial list small. No group should be made up of more than twelve people. At first, six or eight might be better, but do limit the group to twelve members. Beyond that number, the group becomes unwieldy.

Invite some of these couples or individuals, as the case may be, to your home to discuss the idea of a support group. Tell your own story. The others will likely identify with you readily. Explain your feeling of a sense of the need for the support a group could give. To get started, such a group could use this book as a study guide, reviewing one chapter at each meeting but letting discussion flow from the review of the chapter.

Some ground rules need to be suggested and accepted.

1. The group will meet once a week at an agreed-on time and day, preferably during the evening so that husbands and wives who work outside the home can attend.
2. Members must commit themselves to the group as a significant priority, and to the meeting time, allowing

nothing else to prevent attendance (short of illness or an emergency).

3. The meeting place will be rotated among the homes of the members.

4. One member will be recognized as convener and pre-sider, although this person must be careful not to domi-nate the group's discussions. This person will open and close each meeting, keep the group on track, make assignments when a book is to be studied (to be read in advance), and establish the next meeting place at the end of each meeting.

5. *Anything* personal discussed in a group session is to be considered strictly *confidential*, never to be mentioned outside of the group to anyone else. Members must feel free to talk within the group.

6. Group meetings must begin on time and terminate on time (e.g., 7:00 to 9:00 P.M.). If anyone wants to stay longer, they may, but others need to feel free to leave.

7. The group will establish calendar boundaries as well (e.g., September 1 to June 1). Some flexibility needs to be allowed during certain weeks when the group will not meet (e.g., holidays, vacations, unavoidable special events).

What takes place during group meetings? Again, the group decides at its first meeting, allowing for flexibility. Here are some suggestions. Use the first couple of sessions to discuss the group's purpose and ground rules, and to get acquainted. Several of the books listed in Appendix B offer some helpful pointers for beginning.[2] If the group decides to use this (or a similar) book for background reading, the sessions could

2. See William Bangham, *The Journey into Small Groups* (Memphis, TN: Brotherhood Commission, S.B.C., 1974), chapter 4; William Clemmons and Harvey Hester, *Growth Through Groups* (Nashville: Broadman, 1974), chapter 6; Samuel Southard, *Your Guide to Group Experience* (Nashville: Abingdon, 1974), chapter 4.

be composed of a brief review of a chapter by one of the members, followed by group discussion. The questions at the end of each chapter may prove helpful for starting a discussion.

In time a trust level of some depth will probably develop within the group. How soon this develops will depend on the willingness of the members to take the risk. This could take a couple of months of weekly meetings. The deeper the trust level, the more comfortable each group member will feel about discussing his or her family situation. As members begin to share, others will be encouraged to offer evaluation, insights, relevant personal experiences, questions and answers dealing with the point at hand, as well as personal commitments of support, encouragement, and prayer.

Some structure may be needed for group sessions. It is never out of place to open and close group sessions with prayer. If a book is being used for background reading, the first fifteen minutes of each session could be given to a review or evaluation by someone designated in advance. But the remainder of the time should be used for group discussion. The presider needs to be someone familiar with group dynamics, who will keep the discussion flowing and keep the group on the subject, but who does not allow one or two members to dominate the group. Everyone there is hurting and wants help. Although some members may not want to participate actively at first, those with hesitations about talking should be respected but eventually gently encouraged to participate if possible. Even then, it may take some people months to open up. Be patient with them.

When a group reaches its termination date, it should decide its future. Some groups find the experience so meaningful that they continue indefinitely, terminating only during the summer months. Others feel that they accomplished their objectives and no longer meet after this date.

Beware of certain dangers in groups. Determine in advance that your group will *never* become a complaint session about "what's wrong with the church or the pastor," a substitute for church attendance, a clique that shuts out other people from your friendship circle, a therapy group for members who have unusual emotional problems which require special medical, psychological, or psychiatric care, or an effort to solve all the problems of all the members of the group (the group is not a cure-all for the members).

Sharing the Pain

Wounded parents can be a great help to one another. A support group is only one way to help, but a group does provide an opportunity for people to share their pain and find resources for healing. A support group is neither magic nor a complete answer to people's problems. It should be seen only as a temporary life-support system. Eventually you have to breathe on your own.

Sharing your pain helps you to get things out into the open where you can take an objective look at them: conflicts, disagreements, expectations, disappointments, defeats, resentments, anger. Also, sharing your feelings helps you to understand those feelings by allowing other people to reflect back to you what they are hearing. You will see some things about yourself that were hidden before you began to talk.

Art and Betty Collins joined a support group at the same time that their daughter Irene began attending an alcoholic-recovery group. As a result, several insights about themselves came to light. They realized they had been too busy to include Irene in their lives. They wanted her and yet did not have time for her. Art discovered how aloof he was from both her and Betty. Essentially a loner, Art was afraid of intimacy and expressions of affection. Betty learned of her deep feelings of inadequacy as a mother. Consequently, both parents had withdrawn from Irene, who felt abandoned to her own private world. Alcohol offered her a narcotic for the pain of her loneliness. The Collinses gradually began to recognize the need for Irene to be included, accepted, and wanted in the family circle.

Sharing the pain also makes it easier to bear. This is not to suggest that pain should or can always be avoided. Pain is a part of life. It has its lessons to teach. But there is an eventual need for relief. While on the one hand there is a sense in which each person "will have to bear his own load" (Gal. 6:5), there is also, on the other hand, the principle of "bear one another's burdens, and so fulfil the law of Christ" (Gal. 6:2). Mutually sharing the pain of parental discouragement is one way to fulfill Christ's law of love.

Strength in a Community of Faith

Wounded Christian parents bound together in the fellowship of a support group have a unique opportunity to provide strength for one another within their community of faith. There is strength in the shared wisdom, the shared psychological insights, the shared parenting skills, and the shared common concerns, but there is greater strength to be found in sharing your lives in a fellowship of faith.

When wounded Christian parents relate to each other in a support group as fellow Christians, praying for each other, encouraging each other, correcting and teaching each other, an unusual strength is provided. This strength can be found nowhere else, and motivates one to grow as a Christian parent and to be the kind of parent your children need at this time in their lives.

Outside of a support group of other Christian parents, there is also strength provided through your involvement in your church, that wider community of faith. The ministry of your pastor, through both his counseling and preaching, and that of other church staff people, the church's educational program and library resources, Bible-study classes, special family-life workshops, as well as numerous involvement activities, provide spiritual resources that can strengthen your home life.

Confessional Witnessing

How you respond to a wayward son or daughter will have an immeasurable influence on numerous people: other children in the family, relatives, friends, work associates, fellow church members, possibly several unchurched people who know you, not to speak of that son or daughter gone astray. This is a time of testing for your faith. The way you respond to disappointment as a parent will say a great deal about the nature of your relationship to God.

If you will allow God to use this situation to work through the problems you are facing, it can be an unusual opportunity for God to reveal Himself in a most powerful way to those who are watching how you respond. I have known of several wounded Christian parents who have told their stories time and again to interested people and have related how God continued to bless within their homes. Even in the midst of seemingly tragic circumstances, God was able to bring about miracles between parents and children. People do not ignore that type of witnessing. Such shared faith is never artificial but has the ring of reality.

From Suffering to Blessing

Sometimes suffering seems pointless. A life wasted by a son or daughter appears utterly meaningless. But God is able to take suffering, heartache, pain, and disappointment, and turn them into blessings. This is rarely done overnight. We may have to look back months or years later to see what God has been doing. Yet it is the perspective of faith that enables wounded Christian parents to affirm with Paul that "in *everything* God works for good with those who love him . . ." (Rom. 8:28; italics mine).

One blessing I have already alluded to is that wounded Christian parents can many times be sources of comfort, strength, and reassurance to other wounded parents. We need to remember that the God we know in Jesus Christ is the "God of all comfort, who comforts us in all our affliction, so that we may be able to comfort those who are in any affliction, with the comfort with which we ourselves are comforted by God" (II Cor. 1:3–4).

God has given to each Christian the power to bless. As a matter of fact, although primitive religion has known a great deal about the power to curse, one of the unique contributions of the Judeo-Christian faith, beginning with Abraham, was the power to bless.[3] Telling others how God has helped you through your own suffering can be an immense source of encouragement to other wounded parents.

There are several things you can do to turn your suffering into blessing. You can increase your ability to care for others by developing specific skills (e.g., being available, getting involved, communicating concern through listening and responding, reaching out to people who hurt, praying for others). You can develop a ministry of friendship. You can be a friend when a family needs a friend.[4]

By becoming a wounded healer, you will be pouring purpose and meaning into all that has happened to you as a wounded parent. Just be certain to unwrap and rewrap your own wounds "one at a time" so you can be ready for the moment when you will be needed by other wounded parents. Your power to bless is partially the result of the fact that you, too, are wounded. But experience has proven to me and several other wounded parents that there is an unexpected source of healing to be found for oneself in exercising this power to bless, in performing the role of the wounded healer.

Questions for Discussion

1. How do you feel when you discover other wounded parents in your church or circle of friends?

3. Myron C. Madden, *The Power to Bless* (Nashville: Abingdon, 1970), p. 7.
4. See an especially helpful book on this subject by C. W. Brister, *Take Care: Translating Christ's Love into a Caring Ministry* (Nashville: Broadman, 1978).

2. What does it mean to be a wounded healer? Have you known such people?
3. If you are in a support group, how has the experience helped you thus far?
4. What is meant by a trust level? Where is this level in your group?
5. Assess the strengths and dangers of a support group. Which outweigh the others?
6. Is confessional witnessing a viable possibility for you? How can you witness?
7. What are some ways you can turn suffering into blessing?

11

A Theology for Wounded Parents

Wounded parents often ask, "Why did this happen to us?" In many instances what they are really asking is, "Why did *God allow* this to happen to us?" After parents live a Christian life before the children, offer them the advantages of a Christian home, and involve the family in the life of the church, it doesn't seem fair for God to allow children from such a home to stray away morally and spiritually. Such parents eventually develop a theological problem. This chapter is an attempt to address that problem.

God's Experience As a Wounded Parent

As this book has grown in recent years, as I have worked with several wounded parents as their pastor or Christian counselor, and as I have matured in my own sojourn as a parent, it has been a great source of comfort and understanding to discover that God Himself has had personal experience as a wounded parent. The story revealed in the Bible is partly a story of God's disappointments with His children. God is no stranger to the experiences of wounded parents. He understands exactly what you, a wounded parent, are going through.

The concept of the fatherhood of God is found throughout the Bible. (Incidentally, "Father" was Jesus' favorite term for God.) God is the Father of all mankind in the sense that He created the human race (Isa. 64:8; Mal. 2:10). God's nature is like that of an ideal father: He disciplines His children (Deut. 8:5; Prov. 3:11–12); He has compassion for His children (Ps. 103:13); He offers special fatherly care to the fatherless (Ps. 68:5; James 1:27) and to the homeless (Ps. 68:6); He provides for His children their basic needs (Matt. 6:25–33); He comforts His afflicted children (Isa. 66:13). He is our heavenly Father who hears our prayers (Matt. 6:9) and forgives the forgiving (Matt. 6:14). However, God's spiritual fatherhood, involving personal salvation, is possible only through faith in Jesus Christ (Gal. 3:26; 4:1–7).

In a special sense, God is revealed in the Old Testament as the Father of Israel and of the messianic lineage of David (II Sam. 7:4–17; Ps. 89:1–37; Jer. 31:9). However, it was in the relationship of God and Israel that God experienced again and again the heartache, disappointments, and pain of a wounded parent.

Israel was often going astray, chasing after other gods, and committing all sorts of immorality. The sins of Israel are recounted many times, especially in the writings of the prophets, which depict the broken heart of a father because of his wayward children (Isa. 64:1–12; Jer. 3:1–3,19–20). This wounded Parent of Israel, however, used every means possible to bring His wayward children back to Him (Jer. 3:21–25, especially v. 22a, " 'Return, O faithless sons, I will heal your faithlessness.' "). The pleading of God the Father for His children gone astray is truly heartrending (see Jer. 31:15–22). He expresses His disappointment in Israel: "A son honors his father. . . . If then I am a father, where is my honor?" (Mal. 1:6).

However, God expressed confidence that someday a remnant of His wayward children would return to Him (Jer. 31:1–9, 15–17). In II Corinthians 6:16–18, it is revealed that this remnant found its ultimate fulfillment in the church of Jesus Christ. In this passage, Paul combines several Old Testament prophetic statements (Lev. 26:12; Isa. 52:11; Jer. 31:1, 9; Hos. 1:10) to say, "What agreement has the temple of God with idols? For we are the temple of the living God: as God said,

> 'I will live in them and move among them,
> and I will be their God,
> and they shall be my people.
> Therefore come out from them,
> and be separated from them, says the Lord,
> and touch nothing unclean;
> then I will welcome you,
> and I will be a father to you,
> and you shall be my sons and daughters,
> says the Lord Almighty.' "

To this day, God has not abandoned His children, Israel, in that He continues to call them to return to Him through the message of the gospel (Rom. 9–11). This gospel is the story of the wounded heavenly Father whose Christ was wounded for the wayward children's transgressions. Paradox of paradoxes, it is by these wounds that the healing of reconciliation comes (Isa. 53:5; I Peter 2:24). Therefore, God's experience as a wounded parent offers us, as wounded parents, the supreme model for redemptive healing for broken relationships: God was in Christ reconciling the world unto himself (II Cor. 5:19).

If wounded Christian parents will pattern their responses to their children's behavior after the example of Christ—a selfless, sacrificial love that willingly suffers with a faith that God will turn their present defeat into His ultimate victory—then "they shall see their offspring and shall prolong their days; the will of the Lord will prosper in their hands;

they shall see the fruit of the travail of their souls and be satisfied" (author's paraphrase of Isa. 53:10b–11a).

Jesus' Experience with Parental Discouragement

Jesus, of course, never married and was not a parent, but the Gospel records indicate that He knew something of the emotions described by the phrase *parental discouragement*. Several examples suggest this.

Matthew 23 records one of Jesus' major messages, given publicly in the precincts of the temple in Jerusalem. At one point in His speaking, He turns to address the scribes and Pharisees specifically. In the tone of a prophet of God, Jesus sets forth several "woes" of judgment on their rebellious and immoral behavior and attitudes. Finally, He broadens His audience to include the entire city of Jerusalem, not only its current residents and religious leaders, but also a vast sweep of Israel's history in this city:

> O Jerusalem, Jerusalem, killing the prophets and stoning those who are sent to you! How often would I have gathered your children together as a hen gathers her brood under her wings, and you would not! Behold, your house is forsaken and desolate. For I tell you, you will not see me again, until you say, "Blessed is he who comes in the name of the Lord." [Matt. 23:37–39]

Such words truly reflect the feelings of God toward wayward Israel, and here Jesus sums them up and reveals the heart of God. But notice the metaphor of the hen and her scattered brood. This is a parental figure and vividly reflects the grief of a wounded parent whose wayward children stubbornly "would not" return and be reconciled. Such picturesque language suggests strongly that Jesus knew, in His own experience as the Messiah, what a wounded parent experiences.

Another instance of Jesus' experience with parental discouragement is suggested in the parable of the prodigal son (Luke 15:11–32). The way Jesus told this story (as He spoke about the feelings of a father whose son strays away, wasting his life) makes me wonder whether Jesus was possibly revealing something of His own heart toward the wayward.

This is merely speculative, but in all likelihood Joseph died before Jesus left home. As the elder brother, Jesus would have taken Joseph's place as the head of the home, assisting Mary in rearing the other children to adulthood. If one of Mary's other children had strayed away morally and spiritually, Jesus would have carried out the role of the father. If Jesus taught out of His experience as well as insight, such speculation is not too improbable. Certainly Jesus' life reflected the feelings and attitude of the father in this story. He must have known something of what a father feels when a son goes off into a far country to squander his life in loose living.

Two other instances of Jesus' experience with parental discouragement were the cases of Judas Iscariot and Simon Peter. A rabbi would often relate to his small band of disciples much as a father would to his sons. When Judas betrayed Jesus and Simon denied Him publicly, it is obvious that Jesus experienced deep disappointment in them.

Judas, out of greed and possibly resentment toward Jesus for not turning out to be a political and military Messiah, betrayed his master into the hands of the Sanhedrin (Matt. 26:14–25, 45–56; 27:3–10). Simon Peter, out of fear for his own life, refused to admit any knowledge of or association with Jesus following Jesus' arrest by the authorities (Matt. 26:69–75). Both turned their backs on Jesus at a critical moment. Although all the disciples forsook Jesus and fled at the time of his arrest (Matt. 26:56b), Judas and Peter are highlighted in the Gospel story. Judas destroyed himself, never to return (Acts 1:15–26); Peter returned to lead the early church following Jesus' resurrection (John 21:15–23; Acts 1–2).

The word *tempted* in the New Testament can sometimes be translated as "tested." Keeping this in mind, Hebrews 2:17–18 can be applied here. The writer of Hebrews suggests that Jesus was made like us in every respect. He Himself has suffered and been tested as we have in order that He might be able to help us. Consequently, as Hebrews 4:15–16 explains, we do not have a Savior who is unable to sympathize with our weaknesses, but one who in every way has been tested as we are, yet without sinning. Because Jesus knows something of the ordeal of a wounded parent, then with confidence we can draw near to God's throne of grace to receive mercy and find help in our time of need.

Paul's Experience as a Wounded Parent

Whether the apostle Paul was ever married is still debatable. He certainly related to his converts and missionary associates much as a parent does to a child. He addressed Timothy as "my true child in the faith" (I Tim. 1:2) and even had him circumcised as a Jewish father would, although for reasons of witnessing (Acts 16:3). Paul did not hesitate to call Timothy "my son" (I Tim. 1:18; II Tim. 2:1), "my beloved child" (II Tim. 1:2), or "my beloved and faithful child in the Lord" (I Cor. 4:17).

Paul also looked on the members of his churches as his children in the faith. He was their spiritual father. Notice particularly how he addressed the Corinthian church: "I do not write this to make you ashamed, but to admonish you as my beloved children. For though you have countless guides in Christ, you do not have many fathers. For I became your father in Christ Jesus through the gospel. I urge you, then, be imitators of me" (I Cor. 4:14–16).

It was certainly with the church at Corinth that Paul experienced the pains of a wounded parent. The church was divided and its members argumentative and in some cases arrogant and even sexually immoral. Some were taking others to court. Some were abusing their spiritual gifts. Others were offending new converts by eating meat that had been offered to pagan idols. Several were overeating and getting drunk at the church fellowship meals and when observing the Lord's Supper. Certain women were insulting their husbands with their new Christian freedom. Some of the members were even denying the resurrection of the dead. Second Corinthians (especially chapters 11–13) reflects much of his frustration with them. He wrote as a parent writes to his wayward children (12:14–15).

Paul also experienced great parental heartache over the Galatian church's reversion to the legalism of Judaism. He wrote to the Galatians as a wounded parent, pleading with his wayward children to return to their true faith (see especially Gal. 1:6–9; 3:1–5; 4:8–11). Paul's deeply-wounded parental spirit comes out vividly as he writes, "My little children, with whom I am again in travail until Christ be formed in you! I could wish to be present with you now and to change my tone, for I am perplexed about you" (4:19–20).

Moreover, Paul knew disappointment as a spiritual parent when an important young missionary associate deserted him on their first missionary journey. John Mark had gone along to assist Paul and Barnabas (Acts 13:5), but at Perga in Pamphylia John Mark left them and returned to Jerusalem (Acts 13:13). Paul later expressed his sense of disappointment, even resentment, over Mark's cowardly behavior (Acts 15:36–41), so much so that Paul and Barnabas chose to go their separate ways on the next journey. Years later, Paul and Mark reconciled their differences, and Paul, in his last letter, instructed Timothy to "get Mark and bring him with you; for he is very useful in serving me" (II Tim. 4:11; cf. Col. 4:10).

Paul also knew parental disappointment when his associate Demas (Col. 4:14; Philem. 24) deserted him because Demas was "in love with this present world" (II Tim. 4:10).

In all of Paul's disappointments he reflected the compassion, firmness, and optimism of his Lord. In dealing with the wayward Corinthians, he could chide them and still tell them he loved them (II Cor. 11:7–11). He rebuked yet did not condemn them (II Cor. 6:14—7:1; 7:3). He could honestly express his disappointment in them (II Cor. 2:1–4) but also tell them, "I have great confidence in you; I have great pride in you . . ." (II Cor. 7:4). Paul's letters offer a helpful model for wounded parents to follow in relating to their children.

God's Continuing Parenthood

God loves your children infinitely more than you do. He has their best interests at heart. He will not abandon them or forsake them because of their behavior. Your children were God's gifts to you, and if you have given them back to God in prayer, you can trust Him to do His loving best to guide them back into the paths of righteousness.

The psalmist had such abiding faith in God's continuing parenthood that he could say that even if his father and mother forsook him, the Lord would take him up (Ps. 27:10).

If, as Christian parents, you once dedicated your children to the Lord, and in recent years one of them has gone astray, he or she is not out of God's reach. He knows where that son or daughter is, what he or she is doing and thinking, and will not abandon that child. He will continue His watchful care, His pursuit, His calling to return, and His loving provision.

Although the influence of our parenting may be blocked by circumstances and rebellious rejection, God's continuing parenthood cannot be stopped by wayward children.

The Freedom of Man and the Sovereignty of God

All through the Bible, it is clear that God has given to each one of us the freedom to choose, to make our own decisions. If one is to be free to do the right, one must also be free to do the wrong. Your child had the freedom to do whatever he or she did. Why a son or daughter chooses a lifestyle that disappoints his or her parents is another, often unanswerable question. But he or she was free to choose.

You would not want it any other way. No parent wants robots for children, any more than God wants humans to be robots. Love is meaningless if it is not freely chosen. Obedience and respect are empty decisions if not freely made.

When God made man, He ran a tremendous risk, as the story of the Garden of Eden reveals. Likewise, when you and I chose to have children, we ran a great risk. This is life, and the way it ought to be. Therefore, we must accept reality, both its positive and negative aspects, if we are going to be mature and responsible people.

But I have good news for you. Christian parents have the unique privilege to be in the sovereignty of God. Regardless of the seemingly wasteful, stupid, dangerous, ungrateful, foolish, and immoral decisions humans may make, God is still sovereign Lord. Our actions, whether as parents or children, cannot overrule God's sovereign control. Although God will not overrule our own wills, He will always have the last word, whether of judgment or grace or both.

God is creator, sustainer, and Lord of all the universe. For Christians, He is our Savior, Lord, and King. He has not lost control of the world or of our family situation. Regardless of how dark things look in your home, God is still sovereign. We can trust Him to work things out, although it will be with His methods and on His timetable. The God revealed in Jesus Christ can be the Alpha and the Omega, the first and the last, the beginning and the end (Rev. 1:8, 17) of your particular family dilemma. Regardless of what has happened, is happening, or will happen between you and your children, you can still hold on to the sovereignty of God.

One of the greatest affirmations of the sovereignty of God is Psalm 23. Read it every day for the next four weeks. Its faith will be contagious.

A Puzzling Passage

A verse from the Bible that has caused much confusion and perplexity for many wounded parents is Proverbs 22:6, "Train up a child in the way he should go, and when he is old he will not depart from it."

The words "the way he should go" literally mean "according to his way," that is, according to the child's personality, temperament, and aptitude. This proverb teaches that parental instruction should take into account the child's individuality and inclinations. Moreover, such instruction should be given with the child's current degree of physical and mental development in mind.

The *Good News Bible* offers a helpful translation: "Teach a child how he should live, and he will remember it all his life." This verse suggests only that early training is important, and that it will have long-term consequences.

This verse is no guarantee that your definition, instruction, and example of the Christian life will cause your children to turn out just as you want them to. It offers no prophetic promise that if we take them to Sunday school and church as children that all will turn out to our liking. It does not promise that there will be no rebellion, conflict, or differences.

This verse simply reminds us that the early formative years of a child are the time to provide him or her with our best teaching and example, and that he or she will never forget it. But this influence does not overrule the freedom of that child's own will or responsibility for his or her decisions. Our responsibility as parents is to do our best under God and trust Him to bring His will to pass in light of the child's unique personality and God's purpose for that life.

The God of Hope and Comfort

Wounded parents have to have hope in order to survive. Without hope, some of us would quickly despair. The only place to find hope for a perplexed family situation is with

God. He is the God of hope, and His Word is a marvelous stimulator of hope for discouraged parents.

A verse from Jeremiah comes to mind:

> There is hope for your future,
> says the LORD,
> and your children shall come back
> to their own country. [Jer. 31:17]

In addition, God is the God of comfort for parents in pain. Yet there is a sense of divine purpose added to our suffering when God is allowed to deal with it. The God of comfort comforts us in order that we might be able to comfort other wounded parents with the same comfort with which we ourselves are comforted by God. And just as we are sharing abundantly somehow in Christ's sufferings (He identified with us), "so through Christ we share abundantly in comfort too" (II Cor. 1:3–5). Consequently, the God of hope and comfort who is revealed in Jesus Christ enables us to go on living and become wounded healers.

Questions for Discussion

1. How is God's experience as a wounded parent helpful to you?
2. Does Jesus' experience with parental discouragement offer any guidelines for your situation?
3. How is Paul's experience relevant to you?
4. How do you balance the freedom of man with the sovereignty of God in your family situation?
5. Study various translations of and commentaries on Proverbs 22:6. How do you apply this verse to your experience?
6. How do you feel about the future in your family? Why? Do you have any plans for growth and improvement?

12

Postscript
Redemption and Prevention

This final chapter is basically a summarizing set of guidelines for either (1) parents already in the wounded condition or (2) parents who want to prevent becoming wounded. The first section will be a redemptive strategy, while the second will deal with preventive techniques. Most readers will fall into the first category, their situation being somewhat "after the fact," and this will recap in a nutshell much of what the entire book has been saying. I have talked with many young couples whose children are quite small and for whom there simply hasn't been enough time for serious parent-child conflict to develop. Yet these parents are deeply interested in learning how to prevent becoming victims of the wounded-parent syndrome. For them I will offer several suggestions also.

Summarizing a Redemptive Strategy

1. *If you are already a wounded parent, remember that you are not alone.* Your situation is unique. Your story is *your*

story and no one else's. But many other parents all around you are equally wounded and hurting deeply. They need help also, help that possibly you can give out of your own experience. This is a common problem in many Christian homes. The biblical story of the prodigal son speaks to many parents today who have a prodigal son or daughter. Without choosing it you have joined a fellowship of suffering.

2. *It does little good to try to figure out what went wrong.* Usually only God knows the answer, and you cannot go back and relive the past anyhow. Simply reach out to help other hurting parents who live all around you. In addition, get busy on making constructive changes in your own life. If you begin to change, your children will eventually see the difference, and this in time can have a tremendously beneficial effect on their lives. And even if the family situation doesn't improve, at least the positive change in your life will have been worth it.

3. *Release your rebellious child into God's hands.* Turn loose and trust God. I know this is very difficult to do. Parents have a natural inclination, almost an inborn drive, to want to hang on for dear life, believing that any solution or hope of eventual reconciliation depends on their control and direct involvement. However, I have learned that God works best when we get out of the way and trust Him to do what only He can do. Then, be patient. Solutions and reconciliation take time. God wants to work His redemptive transformations in His own time schedule. Besides, God's timing is always better than ours. Remember, He sees the total picture; we see only a fragment.

4. *In the meantime, learn to control your emotions.* Feelings are powerful—for good or for ill. Emotional energy must be channeled by a cool head at the wheel. You are in charge of your feelings. Yes, you are! Each one of us chooses our reactions. Consequently, choose the more constructive and healthy feelings. If necessary, go back and re-read chapter 4. Reconditioning our emotional responses is

hard work, and it takes practice. It often helps to talk out one's feelings with a trusted confidant and/or counselor. Among other benefits, this helps to "get a handle" on our emotions and steer them in a constructive direction.

5. *Stop playing the blame game.* It goes nowhere. There are no winners in this game. The human psyche so often wants to blame someone else for life's problems. None of us is smart enough to know who is to blame, if anyone actually is. Trying to place the blame simply delays one's own growth process in bringing about constructive change. Be willing to take responsibility for yourself so far as determining what your involvement has been in the family situation. Let God take care of all the other people in your life. Focus on what you can do about *you.*

6. *Avoid comparing your children with other children—* your family "mess" with other families' "bliss," your failures with others' successes. Such comparisons are counterproductive and will drive the prodigal farther away.

7. *Never play the "what if" game.* It also goes nowhere because there are no winners here. This is a self-punishing fantasy ("What if I had been a better mother?") or an accusatory rationalization ("What if you had been a better father?"). Nothing constructive can come of such tactics.

8. *Seek individual or family counseling from a competent and trained counselor.* Don't try to "go it alone." Seek help from a skillful counselor especially on how to keep the lines of communication open, with the emphasis placed on learning some listening skills. Shrink your mouth and grow big ears! Never be ashamed to ask for professional help. If you broke your leg, you would seek a good orthopedic doctor, right? If your family relationships are in need of repair, then seek a professional counselor who has good relationship-repair skills.

9. *Work at maintaining and enriching a healthy marriage.* The best thing parents can give to their children is a good marriage. Yet this takes hard work and intentional effort. Being a wounded parent in itself is usually, at least to some

degree, hard on one's marriage. Concentrating on maintaining a healthy marriage provides strength and confidence for a couple experiencing pain with a prodigal child. One way to nurture and strengthen your marriage is to get involved in marriage-enrichment experiences. A growing number of churches are now providing marriage-enrichment retreats at least once a year. Ask your pastor about scheduling one of these.[1]

10. *Organize a support group for wounded parents.* Share the pain and learn from one another. Chapter 10 provided the details on how to do this. One of the values to be discovered in a small support group is that of enabling persons to reach the deeper levels in interpersonal relationships. These levels are caring, sharing, and intimacy. My book *We Need Each Other* provides a road map for reaching these deeper levels.[2] My wife and I discovered them in the context of a small support group. Living on these deeper levels not only strengthened our marriage but also opened doors for better communication with our children.

11. *Grow spiritually and develop a new self-image.* Being a wounded parent is very hard on one's self-image and self-esteem. Self-image is the way you see yourself; self-esteem is the way you feel about yourself. Wounded parents tend to sink into a poor self-image and consequently feel very bad about themselves. Spiritual growth is the pathway out of this condition. The journey begins when you learn the art of Christ-centered self-affirmation. My book *Self-Affirmation: The Life-Changing Force of a Christian Self-*

1. An excellent resource for planning a marriage-enrichment retreat is Diana S. Richmond Garland, *Working With Couples for Marriage Enrichment* (San Francisco: Jossey-Bass Publishers, 1983). For a 12-lesson course to be taught in a church educational program, see Diana S. Richmond Garland and Betty Hassler, *Covenant Marriage: Partnership and Commitment* (Couple's Guide and Leader's Notebook) (Nashville: Baptist Sunday School Board, 1987). For individual study, see Cleveland McDonald, *Creating a Successful Christian Marriage*, rev. ed. (Grand Rapids: Baker Book House, 1981), and Diana S. Richmond Garland and David E. Garland, *Beyond Companionship: Christians in Marriage* (Philadelphia: Westminster Press, 1986).

2. Guy Greenfield, *We Need Each Other: Reaching the Deeper Levels in Our Interpersonal Relationships* (Grand Rapids: Baker Book House, 1984).

Image is a guidebook for this kind of growth.[3] Spiritual growth involves looking ahead, not over your shoulder. However, learn what you can from the past so as not to repeat it.

12. *Seek to build a new relationship with your children—become friends.* In most cases, prodigal children are too old for their parents to continue "parenting" them. What they need from parents more than anything else is friendship. This kind of relationship calls for growth that moves one

from control to communication
from judgment to respect
from less talking to more listening.

Try it. These are really your only options for constructive change.

13. *Become a wounded healer.* This is one way to create purpose and meaning in your pain. Remember that the apostle Paul stated that the "God of all comfort . . . comforts us in all our affliction, so that we may be able to comfort those who are in any affliction, with the comfort with which we ourselves are comforted by God" (2 Cor. 1:3–4). As you help others find healing for their parental pain, you will find healing for yourself as well. Besides, being a wounded healer will make you a better friend with your children. Parents who are full of self-pity and resentment over the wayward behavior of their children are so wrapped up in themselves and their pain that they do not make very good friends with anyone. Wounded healers have learned the art of forgiveness, and forgiveness is at the heart of genuine friendship.

Summarizing a Preventive Strategy

No normal person wants to become a wounded parent. We would all like to prevent becoming such, if at all possible. This section will summarize a strategy of prevention. It

3. Guy Greenfield, *Self-Affirmation: The Life-Changing Force of a Christian Self-Image* (Grand Rapids: Baker Book House, 1988).

is aimed primarily at parents of small children in families where there has not yet been enough time for serious parent-child conflicts to arise.

One of the unexpected consequences of the widespread readership of the first edition of this book was the large number of parents who said something like this: "I wish that I had read this book when my children were preschoolers. I think we could have prevented a lot of our problems from emerging as they did." Others said that when they first saw the book's title they felt it wasn't for them, since they did not see themselves as "wounded" parents. Their children were quite small. But friends urged them to read it for preventive reasons. Many "sweet babies" will one day find themselves swirling in the "terrible teens." Consequently:

1. *Early on, make friends with your children.* You don't have to become "buddies" and "pals" and lose your position of authority and parental leadership, but good parenting balances authority and friendship. Learn the art of having fun with your children. Play does not destroy respect for parents but rather enhances it.

2. *Give your children quality time, not the leftovers of a busy life.* Most people are busy and have hectic schedules. It seems there are never enough hours in the day to do all we have to do. Consequently, we have to establish priorities, and at the top of the list should be one's family. If you are too busy to spend quality time with your children, then you are definitely *too* busy.

One minister told me that his list read like this: God, first; the church, second; his family, third. As kindly as I knew how, I responded that he would still be putting God first if he put his family first in meeting their needs. Some ministers have built great churches while neglecting their families. I believe such ministers are failures in God's eyes.

3. *Begin early to control your family television.* The TV is not all bad; there is much good we can gain from it. However, there are many secular, materialistic, and ungodly values that come across the screen daily. Just as

we protect our children from exposure to disease, bad food, and contaminated water, so should we protect them from daily doses of violence, sexual immorality, greedy and materialistic role models, and the other anti-Christian values communicated through many programs on television.

My wife and I were among the first generation of parents to raise children with a television in the home. Because we had no idea what moral power this instrument could have over our children, we were ill-prepared to control and monitor its influence in our home. We wrongly assumed that anything good enough for public viewing on television would be good enough for us. Now we know differently. Parents simply must take charge of the television set and filter out the bad programs while they filter in the good ones. Otherwise children naively assume that if it's all right for Mother and Dad to watch, it's fine for them too. The blunt truth is that television is a powerful molder of values and shaper of moral character. If not controlled, it can be a serious countering agent for the desired childrearing goals of Christian parents.

4. *Teach and model for your children early on how to select friends carefully.* This is a problem for Christians who heed the scriptural command to reach out and witness to non-believers. However, friendships for small children need to be carefully chosen, lest they be unmindfully influenced in a wrong direction. Many youngsters have been badly influenced into drugs, pornography, sex, and bad language by a poor choice of friends. Christians are to be "in the world" but not "of the world." Parental example and instruction go a long way in guiding children to be discriminating in their choice of playmates.

5. *Spend time learning helpful childrearing techniques.* There are many excellent authors whose books on good Christian parenting techniques are readily available. See Appendix A for a recommended list of materials. Ask your local or regional Christian bookstore to help you secure these types of books. It is truly sad to discover that so many parents have never read one book on parenting skills or

attended one lecture on the topic. Every church should offer at least one course a year on parenting. Ask your pastor or Christian education committee to take the lead in providing such opportunities.[4]

6. *As your children grow and mature, gradually release control over them and trust them to be responsible.* Parenting involves a process of building into a child the powers of self-control. Parents cannot forever be hovering over their children, telling them every move to make. You really don't want to do that for the remainder of their lives. You want them to grow up and be responsible for themselves. Therefore, you have to start early: releasing and trusting. There is a big difference between control and guidance. Yes, you "control" a three-year-old headed for a busy street. But you also take time to teach him or her *why* not to play in a busy street. Parenting is a process of moving from control to guidance to freedom.

7. *Set firm yet loving parameters in your home.* Clear boundaries regarding behavior are needed early. There need to be both house rules as well as out-of-house standards. Children become quickly confused and out-of-control when they are permitted to do whatever they please. They easily recognize that such "freedom" does not reflect genuine love. Even though they will inevitably test the boundaries, they will recognize that limits reflect that their parents care about them.

8. *Model in your own life what you expect from your children and be unashamedly Christian about it* (without being "preachy"). Be Christ-centered and church-centered in your lifestyle. Tell your children early on how you came to know God in Christ for yourself. Explain why you take the family to church. Don't assume they understand by some mystical osmosis. Live the goals you want your children to aspire to. If you want them to be honest, truthful, decent, respectful,

4. An excellent course is now available from a Christian perspective: Dixie Ruth Crase and Arthur H. Criscoe, *Parenting by Grace: Discipline and Spiritual Growth* (Parent's Guide and Leader's Notebook) (Nashville: Convention Press, 1986).

loving, prayerful, caring persons, then you must model these character traits in front of them.

9. *Engage in family worship as a regular habit, making it enjoyable rather than a burdensome duty.* The smaller the children, the briefer this time should be, but even infants and toddlers can learn the values of worship time as a family. As the children get older, let them share in the readings, comments, and prayers. When youngsters grow up and look back on these times, they will never forget their spiritual "roots."

10. *Give your children a good marriage as an example.* Happy, well-adjusted, responsible people testify that their parents had a sound marriage. Such a marriage is characterized by respectful love, enjoyable conversation, thoughtful actions, considerate attention, careful listening, and deep commitment to each other. If genuine commitment is present, difficulties and differences can be managed.

The father of one family was a traveling salesman who was out of town most weeks from Monday until Friday. One Monday evening the mother had prepared warmed-up leftovers for dinner. The three sons, ages nine, ten, and twelve, came in and looked at the meal. The oldest son said disgustedly, "Mama, why is it that when Daddy's here you fix the best meals in town; but when Daddy's gone, you feed us this?" With the wisdom of Solomon the mother smilingly replied, "Well, son, it's like this: Your father and I have a permanent commitment; you kids are just passing through!" What a lesson! Those children could always rest assured that their family was going to stay together. Their parents had a solid commitment to each other. That's a good feeling for children to have.

A fourth-grade schoolteacher asked her class to write a short essay on "What I Like About My Home." One boy wrote: "In our home, Mama has a cookie jar full of cookies. We can eat them only with special permission. When Daddy is home, he can eat from the cookie jar anytime he wants to. When Daddy comes in from work, he goes into the kitchen where Mama is fixing supper. Daddy pats

Mama on the rear and gives her a big kiss; you would think they just got married. I like the way my daddy loves my mama. That's what I like about my home."

11. *Learn how to grow spiritually all of your life.* This involves character, attitudes, feelings, and not simply being formally "religious." Such growth models spiritual growth for your children. They will not likely grow any more than you do. Of all the things you teach your children, nothing is more important than what you teach them about God. And the best teaching is done through your personal example.

12. *Discover and relate to the members of your family on the deeper levels of relating mentioned above.* These deeper levels of caring, sharing, and intimacy are thoroughly explained in my book *We Need Each Other.* Talk and action are not enough. Go deeper. If you've been practicing in-depth relating with your children through their early years, when they reach their teenage years they will not be secretive and withdrawn from you. They will continue to see you as a trusted friend and confidant.

13. *Finally, remember that nothing works perfectly.* You may do all the "right things" and still become a wounded parent. Sometimes we simply do not know why a son or daughter reared in a Christian home goes off into "the far country" morally and spiritually. Parents are not always to blame for what their children do or the decisions they make that cause parental pain. You just have to trust God and do the best you can. A good Christian home where Christ's love prevails is still the best place and the best way to rear children.

In 1982 I was interviewed on a national television program. After asking several pertinent questions about why I wrote *The Wounded Parent,* the interviewer asked me, "Dr. Greenfield, how is it that Spirit-filled and godly Christian parents can have a son or daughter become a prodigal morally and spiritually and break their hearts? Many people believe that consecrated Christian homes will not have such problems."

I responded, "Yes, that myth is still floating around in most of our churches: If you are a dedicated Christian, you won't have any problems. That's a myth!"

The interviewer retorted, "Does the Bible say that?"

Then I recounted from the Sermon on the Mount the words of Jesus about the two houses (see Matt. 7:24–27). One was built on sand, and the other was constructed on rock. The rain, floods, and winds stormed against both houses. Both experienced the same stress and strain. But the one on sand fell; the one on rock stood. The houses are not differentiated; they appear the same. The difference? The foundations. Christian homes will experience many of the same problems other homes do, but they have a solid foundation. They have spiritual resources for survival that others don't have.

The interviewer's eyes lit up and he said, "That's pretty good. Jesus said that, didn't he?"

"Yes," I responded, "Jesus said that."

Then he said, "And Jesus is right, isn't he?"

"Yes, Ben, I believe Jesus is right!" The illustration seemed to be a new revelation on this TV program!

Later, my host commented in the dressing room as my makeup was being removed, "That was some response you gave out there on camera."

"Oh?" I said.

"Yeah, we don't hear that kind of explanation very much here. But good Christians do have problems, don't they? And Jesus taught us that, didn't he? And Jesus is right!"

"Yes," I replied, "Jesus is right!"

Questions for Discussion

1. In developing a redemptive strategy to deal with your current situation, what points in this chapter (first section) speak most directly to you and your family?
2. What are some immediate steps you could take to enrich your marriage? How would this help your situation with a wayward son or daughter?

3. Illustrate how you are currently trying to move from control to communication; from judgment to respect; from less talking to more listening.

4. If you are the parent of small children (preschoolers, early grade-schoolers), what steps in the above preventive strategy speak most directly to you and your family?

5. If one of your children was asked at school or church to write an essay on "What I Like About My Home," what would he or she write? Role-play on this one.

6. What behavior characteristics do you expect from your children? List several. Ask your husband or wife if you are modeling these traits very well yourself.

Books About Parenting Techniques

The Wounded Parent is written primarily for parents who wish to do something about themselves. It is not a self-help book about parenting techniques as such. The children of some wounded parents are in their early teens while others are in college or even in their twenties or thirties. This book was designed to help wounded parents regardless of the ages of their children.

However, some readers still have their children at home and are in need of special guidance about childrearing. The following books have been helpful to many parents. No one book is perfect or will address the issues your family is facing. But you should find many helpful ideas and practical suggestions that apply to you and your family situation.

Brazelton, T. Berry, M.D. *Families: Crisis and Caring.* Reading, Mass.: Addison-Wesley, 1989.

145

Bustanoby, Andre. *Being a Single Parent.* Grand Rapids: Zondervan, 1985.

Dinkmeyer, Don, and McKay, Gary D. *The Parent's Handbook: Systematic Training for Effective Parenting.* Circle Pines, Minn.: American Guidance Service, 1982.

_____. *The Parent's Guide: Systematic Training for Effective Parenting of Teens.* Circle Pines, Minn.: American Guidance Service, 1983.

Dinkmeyer, Don, et al. *The Effective Parent.* Circle Pines, Minn.: American Guidance Service, 1987.

Dobson, James. *Hide or Seek: How to Build Self-Esteem in Your Child.* Old Tappan, N.J.: Revell, 1974.

_____. *Parenting Isn't for Cowards: Dealing Confidently with the Frustrations of Child-Rearing.* Waco, Tex.: Word Books, 1987.

Dreikurs, Rudolf, and Soltz, Vicki. *Children: The Challenge.* New York: Hawthorn Books, 1964.

Gordon, Thomas. *P. E. T., Parent Effectiveness Training: The Tested New Way to Raise Responsible Children.* New York: New American Library, 1975.

Grant, W. Wayne, M.D. *Growing Parents, Growing Children.* Nashville: Convention Press, 1980.

Hendricks, Howard G., et al. *The Encyclopedia of Christian Parenting.* Old Tappan, N.J.: Revell, 1982.

Juroe, David J. and Bonnie B. *Successful Step-Parenting: Loving and Understanding Stepchildren.* Old Tappan, N.J.: Revell, 1983.

Ketterman, Grace H., M.D. *You and Your Child's Problems: How to Understand and Solve Them.* Old Tappan, N.J.: Revell, 1983.

Leman, Kevin. *Making Children Mind Without Losing Yours.* Old Tappan, N. J.: Revell, 1984.

For parents who are having extreme difficulties with rebellious teenagers, the following books are available.

Dollar, Truman S., and Ketterman, Grace H., M.D. *Teenage Rebellion.* Old Tappan, N. J.: Revell, 1979.

Kennedy, D. James. *Your Prodigal Child.* Nashville: Thomas Nelson, 1988.

Lewis, Margie M., and Lewis, Gregg. *The Hurting Parent.* Grand Rapids: Zondervan, 1980.

White, John. *Parents in Pain.* Downers Grove, Ill.: InterVarsity, 1979.

For parents with the especially difficult problems of suicide, child sexual abuse, or homosexuality in the family, the following may be helpful.

Hewett, John H. *After Suicide.* Philadelphia: Westminster, 1980.

Peters, David B. *A Betrayal of Innocence: What Everyone Should Know About Child Sexual Abuse.* Waco, Tex.: Word Books, 1986.

Switzer, David K. and Shirley A. *Parents of the Homosexual.* Philadelphia: Westminster, 1980.

Appendix B

Books About Small Groups

Barker, Steve, et al. *Good Things Come in Small Groups: The Dynamics of Good Group Life.* Downers Grove, Ill.: InterVarsity, 1985.

Casteel, John L., ed. *The Creative Role of Interpersonal Groups in the Church Today.* New York: Association Press, 1968.

Clemmons, William, and Hester, Harvey. *Growth Through Groups.* Nashville: Broadman, 1974.

Clinebell, Howard J., Jr. *The People Dynamic: Changing Self and Society Through Growth Groups.* New York: Harper and Row, 1972.

Dibbert, Michael T., and Wichern, Frank B. *Growth Groups: A Key to Christian Fellowship and Spiritual Maturity.* Grand Rapids: Zondervan, 1985.

Hendrix, John, ed. *On Becoming a Group.* Nashville: Broadman, 1969.

Leslie, Robert C. *Sharing Groups in the Church: An Invitation to Involvement.* Nashville: Abingdon, 1970.

Peace, Richard. *Small Group Evangelism: A Training Program.* Downers Grove, Ill.: InterVarsity, 1985.

Reid, Clyde. *Groups Alive, Church Alive: The Effective Use of Small Groups in the Local Church.* New York: Harper and Row, 1969.

Southard, Samuel. *Your Guide to Group Experience.* Nashville: Abingdon, 1974.